# The Thrive Life

*Thomas Winterman*

ISBN: 149478128X
ISBN 13: 9781494781286

My journey to living a thrive life did not come about on my own. In fact it was quite the opposite. I never could have accomplished any of this without my number one fan. Thank you to my love, my life, my motivation, my Kristen.

Thank you to Cole; you are the reason for all of this.

A big thank you to all others who helped make this a reality as well. Thank you, Debbie, for your constant encouragement; thank you, Dr. Fitch, Dr. Marshall, and the rest of the faculty at Troy University PC for my world-class education; thank you, Becky, Dad, and the rest of my family for unending support; thank you, Brian and Chris, for your awesome edits; thank you to everyone who helped along the way. This is for you! Thrive on!

# Contents

# Introduction

Every day when you wake up, you are not the same person who rose from bed the previous day. Every day of your life you are either learning and growing or atrophying and wasting away. There are thousands of choices that you make every single day that are shaping the person you will be tomorrow. There is a better version of you inside just waiting to be released! The sad truth is that many people are living mediocre lives and have grown to not only accept the mediocrity but expect it.

I was living a life of mediocrity for many years. I was obese and a community-college dropout. I had trouble keeping relationships and was stuck in a terrible job I hated. Then I had my "ah-ha" moment. I had a moment I will forever remember as the exact point in time in which I took control of my life and said, "Enough is enough." Today I am in the best shape of my life. I have a beautiful family, and I obtained a master's degree in counseling psychology and love going to my job every day!

It all started with my ah-ha moment. My world did not change for me all at once, but every day since my moment I have been improving in some way. Are you tired of being mediocre? Maybe you live a pretty great life, but I guarantee you it can be better. One of the remarkable things about human existence is that there is no such thing as arriving. We continue to strive, work, and grow until the day we pass. No matter where you are in your life, there are always aspects that can be improved. Do you want to be a better parent? How about a better spouse? Would you like to be healthier? Achieve financial peace? Utilizing reality therapy, choice theory, and other counseling techniques, I will show you how to set goals and take control of your own life once and for all!

Let this book be your ah-ha moment, and let today be the first day of becoming the best you possible. Your ah-ha moment will help you get started on your journey, but you will need some help accomplishing your goals. Your guide and strategy for effective change is in the pages that follow.

What is therapy? I used to think that therapy was some sort of mysterious process. First of all, if you went to therapy, you were going to talk about your childhood (whether you wanted to or not) and probably uncover some sort of childhood trauma or Oedipal complex (if you don't know what that is, Google it). You would walk into a well-decorated office, lie down on a couch, and spill your guts. Oh, and the therapist had to wear a suit. Glasses (or a monocle) are a must, and some sort of facial hair is absolutely required. A full beard is preferable—no, crucial. This therapist would be a master of asking questions as he guides you (the client) to the place he wants you to be. The therapist is the expert, and you are there to learn. This is therapy, right? Sort of. This somewhat describes one type of therapy—of course with some exaggerations. Some time has passed since the days of Sigmund Freud, and therapy has undergone a number of transformations. It has evolved. There have been many theories on human personality and functioning and, as a result, many ideas on how people get stuck and how to help them.

Is one theory of counseling/therapy more right than any other? Some would say yes, but the truth is that no one knows definitively. Some theories may be more helpful to certain individuals basically because we are all different and have different preferences. Do you have to lie on a couch? No. Does therapy have to be in an office? No way. Does the therapist have to be a genius? Not a chance. Surely the beard is required, right? Not even peach fuzz. In some theories, you do not even talk about your past at all! There go my preconceived notions about therapy. So, what exactly is therapy?

Ask any therapist that question and you may get a different answer every time. I believe that the goal of therapy is to help a person realize his or her maximum potential and equip them with tools to overcome future roadblocks. The means of achieving this goal are different from therapist to therapist, but I tend to ascribe to my own personal blend of the theories of functioning posed by Dr. William Glasser (reality therapy and choice theory), Steve de Shazer (solution-focused therapy), and Viktor Frankl (existentialism). One of the main points made by these theories that runs contrary to many others is that human beings possess within themselves the ability for change and solutions to their problems. All we need is a push in the right direction and a competent guide through our journey, and then we can all achieve our greatest potential.

The ability to be the best person you can possibly be does not have to be bestowed upon you by some higher power, nor does it take some life-altering tragedy or traumatic experience to bring out the best in you. These are examples of catalysts for change or, as I like to call them, ah-ha moments, and everyone has to find their own. Everyone has within themselves the capacity for greatness. Greatness is not defined as achieving a certain financial status, getting a particular degree, climbing a mountain, giving money to the poor, or raising a family. The amazing thing about greatness is that you get to define it; *you* decide what being great means. You are not confined by someone else's definition of what it means to be great. If you define greatness by climbing a mountain or raising a family, do it! Your limitations are not limitations at all. In fact, they may be the very things that make you unique and inspire others as you begin your journey to find the best you. The solutions are within yourself; you just have to find them. It is OK that you do not have them right now because with this book I am going to help you get there.

You may be wondering if such self-exploration and improvement is somewhat self-absorbed. After all, this book is about *you.* I will touch on our relationships with others and the importance of outside influences, but the crux of the book is personal change. So is it selfish to strive for personal goals? I would flip that line of thinking around; I think challenging yourself to grow and become better is sel*less*. If you have ever flown in an airplane you have no doubt sat through the mandatory safety briefing the flight attendants give before each flight. When they begin talking about the oxygen masks that come down during emergencies, they tell you that adults should secure their own masks first before helping their children. Uhhh, what? That flies in the face of all our basic parental and decent human instincts. Are flight attendants terrible people? No. The reality is that you cannot effectively help someone unless you are healthy and thinking clearly. Put your mask on first; then help others. This book and your self-improvement are your ways of putting on the proverbial mask. Helping yourself become better is not selfish; it is selfless. Selfishness would be to wallow in a mediocre life. Selfishness would be to continue eating and drinking whatever you want without thinking of the consequences. Selfishness would be to take the easy road and live a life that never dares to be amazing. Selfishness is the easy road; selflessness is the path of sacrifice and growth.

My motivation for writing this book was my own life experience and the experiences I have had in working with individuals and families in the mental health field. The concepts and ideas presented in choice theory and reality therapy helped me focus my life and effectively go after my

goals. They have been so effective in helping me and helping the families I work with in achieving goals that I wanted
to share these concepts with the world. Choice theory and
reality therapy provide basic step-by-step walk-throughs on
why we behave the way we do and strategies for changing our
behaviors. The solutions are inside of you! You do not have
to see a therapist to set goals for yourself and start living
more effectively, but I do honestly recommend that everyone
see a therapist for their own mental health. That recommen-
dation may make some people scoff and think, "Therapy?
I don't need therapy! I am doing fine on my own!" I used
to think this as well, but the truth is that none of us gets
through this life and develops the skills we need alone. We
all could use some help from time to time, and there is no
shame in that—only enlightenment.

This book is not designed to treat serious mental illness
and is not a substitute for therapy. If you have a mental illness
you should consult with a therapist on treatment. This book
is designed to help average, everyday people become the best
person he or she can be—the one just waiting to burst out!

So get ready, take a deep breath, and remember who you
are right now; when you are done with this book and have
completed the exercises, you will never be the same again!
Note: When you see "Thrive Work," it's time to grab a pen
and paper. This is where you will be completing exercises to
bring you closer to your thrive life.

# PART I:

## Who Are You

Thank you for deciding to read *The Thrive Life* and joining me on this journey! I guarantee that if you read through this book and apply the principles you will see effective and lasting change in your life.

This portion of *The Thrive Life* invites and encourages you to make an honest and comprehensive self-evaluation. Warning: this part may sting a little because you will admit some things about yourself you do not like, but it is absolutely necessary. It is impossible to become the person you want to be if you do not first truly understand who you are. Think of your quest for a thrive life as a journey. You definitely need to map out where you plan to go before you start moving, but knowing where you are going is not the first step. Before you begin charting a destination, you first have to know where you are.

# CHAPTER 1

# What's Your Name?

Say your name out loud. You might feel silly, and if you're in public, people might look at you weird. But that's OK, we're working on something. Say your name out loud again, and this time, close your eyes and then say it a third time. Let the sound of your voice ring in your ears and really think diligently about your name. What images did you see when you closed your eyes? What thoughts crossed your mind? Are you proud of your name? Did your name elicit happy thoughts ripe with contentment? Or did thoughts of regret and a life poorly lived enter your mind?

Our names are more than just mere labels to distinguish one person from the next one. Our names carry with them a reputation, and, for those who know us, our names bring about very specific images and thoughts. Think about what your name means to your friends, your family, and your coworkers. Is your name something that you're proud of? Whatever your name means, whatever weight it holds, it is your very own creation. You are in complete control over who you are and what your reputation is. For many of us, this is a painful realization—that we are solely responsible for who we are. However, who you are today does not have to be who you are tomorrow. Take charge, make a change, and take control of your identity.

Who are you? At first glance this is such an easy question. No problem. Who am I? Well…I…uh…uh-oh. I thought I knew the answer, but it is not so simple. Sometimes it is OK to struggle to find an answer. Who are you? Such a deep and profound question cannot be answered with a brief sentence or two, can it? We are complex, evolving creatures who exist within different contexts in various phases of life.

Think back to second grade. You were around seven years old, and the world was your oyster. For most, the biggest concern was what choice to make when the ice cream truck arrived. I mean, that strawberry shortcake ice cream cone was amazing, but the baseball glove with the gumball baseball looked pretty awesome. You were not too concerned about your social standing because you were all just kids who didn't know any better yet. You were just you. Maybe you were involved in clubs, sports, or church. Your identity was that of a child. Your job was to be a kid and have fun. Fast forward to your freshman year of high school. Boy, things were different. Your identity was defined in a social context, and you would do anything to protect your reputation. The world was a little intimidating, and you began to feel real pressure to develop not only your social standing but also your academic future. You felt somewhat as if you had grown up, and your worries may have begun to pile up. Compare the person you were in second grade to the one you were when entering high school. Are those two people different? In most cases the answer is definitely yes. The reason for this is that you aged by eight years or so, hit puberty, and started developing into an adult.

Let's skip ahead again. It's today. So, who are you? You are unequivocally, without a doubt the complete and total sum of a lifetime of choices—your choices. Every waking moment we make choices that may very well continue to ripple throughout the entirety of our lives. Sometimes the choice seems simple and may not seem like a choice at all. Chances are you woke up this morning and chose to get out of bed. Sure, there are factors that have influenced your choice, such as taking care of children, getting to work so you do not get fired, or simply protecting your sanity by rising from the bed and doing something with your day. Did you have to get out of bed? No. The point is that there is always a choice.

Now, you are finally out of bed. What are you going to eat for breakfast? That handful of donuts looks good, and it will likely bring about major short-term satisfaction. But what are the long-term effects? Of *one* handful of donuts? The effects are not terrible. However, our choices tend to become habits, and a donut habit can be disastrous for your waistline. Maybe you decide to go with the egg-white and spinach omelet?

That is certainly healthier than donuts, but it won't taste as good. Or maybe you decide to skip breakfast all together. That sounds like a decent decision because you don't really care for breakfast anyway—and as a bonus, no calories! Well, you have probably brought your metabolism to a screeching halt as your body is likely to go into starvation mode. All of these choices, and we haven't made it past breakfast!

Stop and think of the thousands of choices you make every single day. These decisions seem innocent and often require little thought, but they can have far-reaching implications. Remember, choices often become habits. Habits become personality and will ultimately define who we are. Not only do our choices have a profound impact on ourselves, but oftentimes our choices affect others in our life and the world around us.

Whether we want them to or not, our choices and behaviors send messages out to those in the world around us. Sometimes the message is obvious and intentional. When I pick up flowers for my wife, the overt message is "I love you" or maybe "I'm thinking about you." However, what if she specifically had told me that she absolutely detests flowers? Then the message my behavior sends is "I don't really care about you, and I'm going to do what I want." In both instances I brought her flowers, but the messages were "I love you" and "I don't care about you." Those are a little different!

There are more subtle messages sent through our daily choices, even the choices that we think affect no one but ourselves. What messages are you sending others by the life you are living? When people hear your name, what message do they associate with you? The answers to these questions usually say a lot more about who you really are than you could ever articulate yourself. It is entirely possible to unintentionally send a negative message, and it is also possible that the person who received the message has a distorted view of receiving behavioral messages. This is certainly not something to beat yourself up over because you can only control your own thoughts and actions. In the same vein, do not be quick to dismiss his or her feelings as he or she may have a valid point of view. Carefully ponder the majority of the messages you are sending, especially to those closest to you. Then take a deep breath and ask, "Who am I?"

## Thrive Thought:

Wow; that chapter can be a little frightening. Understanding that a) every action you take is a choice, b) those choices accumulate to form a personality, and c) that personality communicates who you are to others likely felt like a huge slap in the face for most readers—it hurt me. However, there is hope, friend. You are completely in control of your choices! By the end of the book, you will have the knowledge, skills, and plan to become the person you want to be. Live, learn, thrive!

# CHAPTER 2

# Who I Was

I was twenty years old, and I was fat. I was really fat. It is so strange to say that now because I used to validate my weight by calling myself "heavy," "big," or "full-framed." Nope; I was fat. Five years of mindlessly chugging sodas and eating whatever I wanted whenever I wanted had caught up with me. I chose to mix those dietary choices with an absolute disdain for anything that remotely resembled exercise, and thus I created the perfect fat recipe. I was literally the unhealthiest person I knew, and knowing what I do now, that was pretty embarrassing. My decisions also had me in a dead-end job that provided no personal satisfaction, a near minimum-wage paycheck, and absolutely no opportunities for advancement. To top off my growing résumé of fantastic decision making? I would sign up for courses at the local community college and then skip class. I paid for those classes and then made the decision to not go. What? I forfeited a scholarship that paid for more than 75 percent of my tuition; I was placed on academic probation; and I was not allowed to register at the college for a short period of time due to failing grades. Looking back now, I think I could have crowned myself the king of dumb. Surely there was someone to blame. Some mysterious illness or maybe a repressed traumatic event, or maybe my parents were mean to me? No, no, no. None of that was true. And even if it had been, I was making the decisions that led me to where I was.

I poured all of my energy and efforts into church. I spent every spare moment there, developing what seemed like the most and only important thing: my spiritual life. In my mind, my actions were justified. What could be more important than your soul? Could there be a nobler venture? To me nothing else mattered. I built my spiritual being at the expense of my body and my mind. My life was completely out of balance, and I made the decision to justify that imbalance. But more on the mind/body/soul balance later. So what happened? What miraculous event saved me from certain death by heart failure (even though I would surely have gone to heaven)? The first step in my journey to wellness was the smile of a beautiful woman. It was the kind of smile that makes your heart skip a beat, the kind of smile that makes you see cartoon birds flutter around and hear sappy '80s love songs. Somehow, some way, she saw through all my flaws and bad decision making, and she loved me. That love blossomed into marriage, and about six months into that marriage I had my ah-ha moment.

It happened all at once one day while I was at work. It was like any other summer day in Florida. I was driving a delivery truck for an electrical supply company, and it was just Wednesday to me. As usual, the temperature was hovering around one hundred degrees with humidity so thick that you could almost reach out and grab a handful of it. I was on my way out of town on my normal route, which was about two hours roundtrip. My ah-ha moment hit me hard and fast. Sitting there in my truck, I was suddenly ashamed of who I was. I said my name out loud, and immediately I was flooded with images of wasted potential. I was driving a truck when I knew it was not the highest point I could reach. I had settled for a job because I was too lazy and too busy at church to develop any occupational skills or learn new skills through school. I had let my body go so far that I was regulated to polo shirts because I was embarrassed by the way T-shirts sat on my stomach and neck. I knew at once where I was headed. I was headed for certain death before age forty because of my eating habits, family history of heart problems, and complete lack of exercise.

I was so embarrassed by every portion of my life. And then a thought occurred to me: what message am I sending to my wife by living my life this way? By not taking care of myself mentally or physically, I was sending her the message that I did not care about her. "That can't be true," I told myself. Of course I cared. I tried to rationalize my thought away. "I love my wife," I told myself over and over. However, my choices spoke louder than any words that could be said, and my choices were saying that I did not care about my own life. Because I did not care about my own life, I did not care about being with her or providing for her. That realization hit me so hard that it hurt. Then, just as quickly, another thought came to me. When we have children, what message will I have sent to them by living my life this way? The message reflected in my choices was that Dad doesn't care about himself and never cared about much. The lessons my behaviors would teach them would be laziness, apathy, and living for self. That hurt worse. That day, that very moment, I made the choice to change. I decided that enough was enough, and I wanted to take control over my life, my name, and the messages I was sending through my choices. The next day I begged and pleaded to be readmitted into college, began a diet, and started prioritizing my life. It's been a long road, but six years later I have my master's degree in counseling psychology, am down eighty pounds, in the best shape of my life, and am experiencing far greater life satisfaction than I ever dreamed was possible.

## Thrive Thought:

Looking back I can see the shame of my previous life. I can still feel the embarrassment and absolute horror about the way I looked, felt, and acted. However, the same detailing of my failures shows me how far I have come. This is something you can do too. Do you have to be wallowing in mediocrity to move toward a thrive life? No way. Anyone in any phase of their life can still make improvements. Your life might be going pretty well and headed in the direction you want; this book is still for you. Hang in there! For those of you making big changes, one day very soon you will be chronicling the person you used to be. Today is the last day of the old you. Thrive on!

# CHAPTER 3

# It Is OK to Not Like Your Name

When you said your name earlier and you really thought about your life and the messages you were sending, did you feel a sense of regret? Maybe you felt as if you could have made some better choices? It is OK to be dissatisfied with where you are. *It is not only OK to be dissatisfied with where you are, but it is also the very first step to real change.* Dr. Robert Wubbolding, a leader in reality therapy, says in his book *Reality Therapy for the 21st Century* that it is categorically impossible for a person to change unless he or she first decides that a change would be advantageous. Recognizing the need for change is a prerequisite for effective change. Do not, I repeat, do not beat yourself up for the choices that you have made up to this point. Anything you have done thus far is done. There is no point in dwelling in the past. Being angry at yourself for past decisions will not bring about effective change. It is not possible to make the best decision in every situation every time. Most people do not walk around thinking of all the choices they have and then purposefully make an unhealthy choice. The truth is that we make the best decisions we can given the information, resources, and support we have at the time. Every decision that is made makes sense to the person who made it at that time.

However, we should be cognizant that the line between being content and complacent is a very thin one. The moment we stop striving, we stop reaching, we stop trying to be better; that's the moment when atrophy strikes. Let's say you have been working your tail off to lose weight and get in shape. You have been eating like a rabbit and watching your food like some sort of calorie-hawk. You have become so neurotic about your health that you are now that obnoxious health nut you swore you would never be. You find yourself saying pretentious phrases such as "Does that have gluten in it?" or "I had a slice of bread this morning and I'm at my carb limit," or "I made the switch from regular cardio to interval training." You have been jogging almost every day. Suddenly, you realize that you have reached your goal. You can jog three miles without seeing your breakfast again, and you have dropped twenty-five pounds! You have arrived! It's time to do your happy dance, eat some cake, and post your success on Facebook for the world to see, right? Absolutely. Revel in your success, enjoy your moment, and invite your friends and family to celebrate with you. However, you had better be prepared to continue working.

Let's say you are so thrilled about your success that you choose to take two weeks off from jogging. The next time you lace up those fancy running shoes, the odds are that you will not be able to pound out those three miles as you had previously. Perhaps you let the diet slip, and you fell back into old habits. Boom; ten of those pounds are back. It is so easy for this to happen, and I know because it has happened to me! Twice! It is human nature to become content with who we are, and sometimes we really do need a break; that's perfectly fine. However, while contentment is OK, it often creeps over the line into complacency. Being content with who you are is fantastic, but since we are always changing, you have to work to stay who you are! Being content is accepting who you are but still choosing to attempt to maximize your potential. Being complacent is choosing to do nothing, and by choosing nothing, you are choosing a version of you that is far below your potential.

**Thrive Thought:**

When it comes to making changes and becoming something great, I was always waiting. Perhaps I was conditioned to believe that greatness would only come after I lost a beloved family member or friend, faced a life-changing illness, was struck with gamma radiation, or given adamantium claws. The truth is that wanting to change is a plenty good enough reason for change. Do not be fooled; the greater your why, the easier the journey may be (more on that later). Trust me, if you keep waiting for your moment to find you, it'll never come. Go and get it!

# CHAPTER 4

# Choice Theory

You have probably noticed that words such as "choice" and "choose" have been used relentlessly to this point. Annoying, isn't it? Ah, but there is a reason. One of the greatest realizations that a person can come to is "I am responsible for my behaviors. I can change myself, but I cannot change other people." This is the crux of reality therapy and the message behind choice theory. There is always a choice. We make literally thousands of choices a day that ultimately shape the version of ourselves we are becoming. Wow. This can be really overwhelming to think about. One reason why people become stuck or have difficulty becoming who they want to be is because so much time and effort is wasted on trying to control things that are not in their control. We are responsible for our behaviors. We can change ourselves, but we cannot change other people.

Have you ever tried to control a three year old? It sounds easy because he or she is so small and we hold so much power over him or her. This is something I thought I could do until I had one. Now choice theory makes a lot more sense to me. Trying to "make" a three year old go to sleep or eat dinner will make you far more exhausted and frustrated than it makes him or her. What can we do then? We manipulate the situation and change the game by controlling our reactions and changing our approach. We quit giving attention to temper tantrums and they magically stop. We create situations that make it more advantageous for the child to eat dinner and go bed – they suddenly comply. Change yourself, change your world. Another frustratingly fruitless endeavor that so many of us engage in is trying to get another person to love us. *You cannot control anyone except yourself.* You will never "make" a person love you. The best way to gain love and respect is to take control of your behaviors and become a person whom it is impossible not to love. It sounds like such a simple concept, but once you grasp it completely, you will realize the power in it.

We (I'm guilty of it myself) tend to blame others or environmental factors for things that happen in our lives, or we tell ourselves they are the reasons that we are not the kind of person we want to be. It is a story that many of us hear, and some of us tell, every single day. "If my boss wasn't such a jerk, I would have received that promotion." Maybe your choice to be consistently late to work cost you that promotion. Perhaps your lack of productivity is something your boss took into consideration. "If my spouse was not so stubborn, our marriage would be so much better."

By taking control of our choices and our behaviors, we can affect change in the people and circumstances around us. Become that person you want your spouse to be, and you will be amazed by the results.

Sure, sometimes life happens to us, and sometimes people wrong us. You cannot control what has happened or what other people do. You can only control your behaviors. If we put all our effort and energy into focusing on our behaviors, creating goals, and becoming the best person we can be, we would be much happier and more successful.

So why do we make the decisions that we do? Sometimes we make completely bone-headed choices even when we know that there is a better option. In order to take control of our decisions, it is important to understand the genesis of our decision-making processes. The answer to why we choose to do what we do is simple and incredibly complex at the same time: it is because we are constantly striving to fulfill our basic human needs. William Glasser, MD, the founder of reality therapy, proposed that all human beings have five basic needs. These needs are general, not specific, and are universal. The needs are love/belonging, power/accomplishment, freedom/independence, fun, and survival.

## Love/Belonging

Love/belonging is the need others in our lives generally fulfill. Our spouse, friends, family members, and coworkers all play a role in satisfying our basic need for love/belonging.

## Power

The need for power typically brings to mind images of a corrupt CEO or Wall Street executive who sacrifices anyone in his or her path to more money and power. However, this is not necessarily the type of power that is a basic human need. The words associated with power in this case would be "accomplishment", "achievement", or "inner control." We can derive a sense of power by completing a task, overcoming an obstacle, or being recognized for something we have done. Power in this case carries with it a very positive connotation.

## Freedom/Independence

Our need for freedom and independence is typically what dominates our minds as teenagers. As we grow older, we still seek to have a sense of autonomy—that is, being able to make our own decisions.

## Fun

Having fun is advantageous in so many ways. It allows us, if only briefly, to leave the stresses of our life behind. Think about all of your favorite moments in your life so far. How many of those thoughts include you having fun? I bet your fondest memories include smiles on the faces of the people in them. It is amazing what a little fun can do for marriages on the fritz or parents who have trouble communicating with their children.

## Survival

The need for survival, or self-preservation, is pretty self-explanatory and is best illustrated by our fight-or-flight response to danger. When faced with imminent danger, our bodies make the decision to run for safety or fight for survival.

These basic needs are the motivation for all human behavior. That sounds simple, but here comes the complex part. We all perceive experiences differently. While roller coasters are fun to me, they may seriously threaten another person's perceived survival need, causing a panic attack or worse. Spending time with your family may fulfill your need for love, but if a person's family is abusive, he or she may have to find love elsewhere. There are an infinite number of scenarios that can highlight the different perceptions people ascribe to need-fulfilling behaviors.

Dr. Glasser proposed that our brain is analogous to a thermostat. When we perceive that one of our needs is not being fulfilled, our brain kicks into gear and generates a behavior to affect the outside world and thereby bring about need fulfillment. Why is it that some people cheat on their spouses? Is it because they are nefarious people who only seek to do harm? Usually not. Perhaps the person's need for love is not being met—according to his or her perceptions—by his or her spouse. Why is it that bullies target those smaller and weaker than themselves? Perhaps they need more power in their lives, and they are desperately trying to get it in any way possible. If you can understand the basic human needs and the fact that we all perceive how to meet those needs differently, behavior does not seem so purposeless. In fact, *all* behavior serves a purpose. Think back on some terrible decisions that you have made in your past. It is easy now to see the error of your ways, but try to think of why you made the decision you did. If you can look back and see your choices in terms of trying to fulfill unmet needs, you may just cut yourself some slack.

---

## Thrive Thought:

It may seem at first glance that an understanding of total behavior is a license to do whatever the heck you want with no consequences at all. After all, "Hey, I was just trying to fulfill my psychological needs" is a pretty sweet argument. Try again! This knowledge provides insight and a reason for past decisions, but it is not an excuse for future idiocy. You know better now. Learn, grow, thrive!

---

# CHAPTER 5

## Reality Therapy Basics

### Perception

When discussing reality therapy—or therapy in general for that matter—the term "perception" often comes into play. Perception is one of those abstract concepts that is easy to define but can be difficult to wrap our minds around and understand. Perception is basically the process of using the senses to acquire information about the surrounding environment or situation. Perception happens quickly, and the unique way that every person perceives the world and others in it is a process that is their own. Every single moment of the day, human beings are taking in information, making judgments about that information (perceiving), and formulating behaviors based on the information and resulting perception. Are you still with me? I know this is some pretty thick theory stuff, but it all ties in, I promise.

# Reality Therapy Basics

Let's say that you grew up in a strictly religious home that believed dancing of any nature was a sin and absolutely forbidden. You attended a wedding, and the time came for the father/daughter dance. As a result of your upbringing and possibly your own value system, you see the act of dancing as sinful and utterly distasteful. Someone who grew up in a more liberal home might have seen this dance as one of the most beautiful moments he or she had ever witnessed. Is one person right and one wrong? No. The dancing is what it is, and it has no intrinsically positive or negative value. The value comes into play through the perception generated by the people who are experiencing the situation.

There is a quote attributed to the author Anais Nin: "We don't see things as they are. We see them as we are." Our perceptions are very much shaped by our childhood, our experiences, and our value system. We can have skewed and irrational perceptions, which tend to be formulated by traumatic events. A person who has been the victim of a robbery may perceive every person he or she sees in a trench coat to be a threat. Perceptions, while they can certainly be misguided, very much create personal and individual realities for all of us.

When we experience something that is found to be need-satisfying (fulfills our need for love/belonging, power/achievement, freedom/independence, fun, or survival) our brain stores that information, and we perceive that experience as being good and helpful. When we have an experience that threatens our needs, we tend to have the opposite reaction: we will not go near that experience again with a ten-foot pole.

Perception plays such a huge role in our lives, especially when determining what kind of person we want to be. We want to be what our own, unique, individual definition of being happy is. No one person can tell you what happiness should be because no one person shares your unique perceptions. Think critically, understand your perceptions and your biases (we all have them), and challenge those perceptions. Meditate upon the things that you have always considered to be reality. Conflict often happens in life because we tend to argue perceptions. Arguing perceptions means there is no right and there is no wrong, only the different ways people view the world. The only time a person's values or perceptions are wrong is when they infringe on the rights of others.

## Total Behavior

When you think of the word "behavior," it usually denotes an action. After all, behavior is usually overt and out front for all to see. I want to challenge your thinking on what "behavior" is. Reality therapy espouses that actions are only one quarter of our "total behavior." Total behavior includes thinking, actions, feelings, and physiology. All of these components are connected and absolutely inseparable. One component does not "cause" the others, but, rather, they coexist. Making a change in one component of total behavior will undoubtedly cause an effect throughout the entire total behavior system.

One of the best ways to understand the topic of total behavior is to use the analogy of a car. The two front wheels of the car are actions and thinking while the back wheels are feelings/emotions and physiology. When driving, you have complete control over the front wheels by using the steering wheel. You do not have direct control over the back wheels, but they must go where the front wheels go because they are connected. Similarly, in whichever direction we steer our thoughts and actions, our feelings/emotions and physiology will follow. Consider the fact that the front wheels (actions and thoughts) are on the same axle. If you want to change what you are doing, you can change your thinking, and if you want to change what you are thinking, you can accomplish this by changing what you are doing. Similarly, the back wheels are on the same axle and have the same type of connectedness. Have you ever noticed that intense emotion is usually accompanied by physiological responses? When you are especially anxious, your heartbeat may pick up speed, your palms might sweat, and your breathing may become shallow and faster. These are physiological responses to feelings/emotions. You can take control over your total behavior car today, right now. Or, you can continue to think and do what you have always thought and done and continue to get what you have always gotten.

## Actions

Actions are somewhat self-explanatory and the easiest component of total behavior to understand. Actions are the things that we do. They are the words we say and the behaviors we engage in. Our actions are the component of total behavior over which we have the most control. Controlling what we do is far simpler than controlling how we think, how we feel, or how we physically react. Our actions a lot of times have a much greater effect on our total well-being than we realize. Did you know that exercise is one of the most commonly prescribed treatments for depression? Taking control and moving one of the front wheels (actions) causes a direct move in the other front wheel (thoughts), and the back wheels (emotions/feelings and physiology) have no choice but to follow.

## Thoughts

Our thoughts are the ideas and images that pop into our head, and we have arguably hundreds of thousands of them throughout each and every day. Henry Ford said, "Whether you think you can or you think you cannot, you are right." I try to meditate on that quote frequently. Our thoughts tend to have a profound impact on the way we perceive ourselves and others. We have more control over our thoughts than we do our feelings and physiology.

One tricky part is distinguishing between what is a thought and what is a feeling. "I feel as if I am a bad friend." "I feel as though I can take on the world today." "I feel like running away and never coming back." "I feel as if I really make a difference with my job." Are those statements thoughts or feelings? Read them again; what do you think? None of those statements actually describe feelings; they all are thoughts. Usually if there is a transition phrase involved, you are experiencing or hearing a thought instead of a feeling. It is natural to hear the phrase "I feel…" and automatically attribute whatever comes next to feelings. Usually feelings will be a couple of words and speak more to a person's state of being rather than ideas.

This is not the easiest concept to grasp, and it may take some time and practice before you can correctly identify thoughts versus feelings. When you are by yourself or listening to others, take note of the way you or someone else speaks when talking about feelings. See if you can determine whether or not he or she is describing feelings or thoughts. Another way to help you distinguish between the two is the number of words used. Feelings only take two or three words usually: "I feel happy," "I feel sad," etcetera.

## Feelings/Emotions

Feelings and emotions are very powerful. Sometimes it feels as if they come over us like a wave and there is nothing we can do to stop them. Have you ever said or done something while experiencing strong emotions and then later wished you could take it back because you were not thinking clearly? I think that has happened to all of us and will continue to happen to humans until the end of time. We are emotional creatures, and emotions are not inherently bad because they can inspire and bring about positive change just as quickly as they can bring about negative change. The problem with emotions is that we often feel as if they are outside of our control and being manipulated by others and the environment.

We are guilty of saying statements such as "She made me mad!" or "My family makes me feel overwhelmed!" Stop and think about those statements for a moment. Is anyone in control of your emotions except for you? The truth is that no person or situation can make you feel a certain way. Take ownership of your feelings and practice using "I" statements. Instead of the above, practice saying, "I feel angry because…" or "I feel overwhelmed because…" This slight shift in the way you view your emotions can be very powerful. Remember, total behavior is connected, and emotions, while they can occur spontaneously, can be controlled by taking a hold of our thoughts and actions.

It is also important to note that there is no such thing as a "wrong" feeling. Feelings happen; they just do. Even if you can look back and say, "Wow, it was really illogical for me to feel that at the time," your feelings are not at all wrong. What is important is that you can recognize your feelings and take control over the thoughts and actions (most controllable aspects of total behavior) that usually accompany feelings and emotions. Do not be afraid to experience your feelings and observe them for what they are. They do not define you and cannot control you unless you allow them to. Too often we get mad at ourselves for our feelings, and that creates a bit of a downward spiral.

Let's say that you and your spouse have a big fight and you need some time to cool off. You leave your house and go for a drive. While driving you ask yourself, "Why do I get so angry every time we talk about this subject? I wish I did not have these feelings. My wife should probably leave me because I am such a screw up." Suddenly, along with your anger, you have now invited in guilt, shame, remorse, fear, anxiety, and a host of other emotions through your thoughts. The chain reaction can be devastating. Your initial anger, justified or not, was the feeling created by the moment. It is *normal* to be angry and upset during an argument with a loved one. Being even more angry and ashamed about being angry is where the downward spiral begins. Pick yourself up, own your initial emotions and feelings, and choose to control your thoughts and behaviors that follow.

Emotions and feelings can be tricky, especially when there are so many of them. How many can you think of? There are most likely thousands of them, and each has its own unique place. Sometimes it can be really hard to pin down what we are truly feeling at any given moment. If you have been married, when you were standing at the altar exchanging vows, what feelings were you experiencing? Most would say happiness, but can you distinguish between feelings of happiness, joy, excitement, overload, anxiety, and fear? Those are just a few of the feelings I remember from that moment in my life. That is why feelings are so difficult to pin down, label, and work on. If I said to you, "Take control of your feelings," you might try, but you would in all likelihood actually be taking control of your thoughts. When you are really focusing on your feelings, try to classify them as good, bad, or neutral.

## Physiology

Let's speak for a moment about physiology. Physiology refers to the internal workings of our bodies—the processes that are usually automatic and mostly outside of our direct control. Through careful introspection and taking control over the other aspects of total behavior, you will find that your physiology is more in your control than you realize. Let's say that it is dinnertime, and you worked so hard today that you skipped lunch. Your body is kicking into gear and telling you that it needs food. The process by which this happens is our physiology.

Our physiology can also be described as a manifestation of symptoms. Let's take worrying as an example. Your spouse is a half-hour late in getting home from work, and suddenly some thoughts start creeping into your head. You may think, "Maybe he [or she] got caught up in work," and you go about your business. Another half-hour passes, and you begin to have more thoughts, such as, "Was there an accident?" You call his or her cell phone and get no answer. Now your thoughts are really starting to take over. You imagine all sorts of worst-case scenarios, and suddenly you cannot think of anything else. Feelings of dread and despair sweep over you as you imagine what could have happened. You have decided that in five minutes, if you do not hear from him or her, you are going to get in your car and go looking. You are worrying so much that you begin to feel physically ill. Your stomach is tensing up and your hands are shaking. Then your spouse comes through the door and says something such as, "Oh, sorry, I got caught up at work and my phone was on vibrate. Whoops." What began as thoughts moved quickly into feelings and then crept its way over to physiology. Even your behavior was affected as you frantically called everyone you could and suspended all other tasks.

In moments such as these, would it be possible to isolate our physiology and take control over the symptoms we are feeling? Perhaps, but it is far more difficult to attempt to do that than it is to attack from another angle. In this instance, your thoughts initiated the total behavior chain of events. If you could take control of your thoughts, rid yourself of the what-if, and focus on what you can control, your total behavior would be affected in a completely different way. Remember, actions and thoughts are the components of total behavior which we have the most control over. Think about what actions could have been done in this scenario to positively affect your total behavior. Perhaps you could have called your spouse's coworker to verify if he or she was still at work. You could have taken action and gone to the workplace, or you could have busied yourself with another task until the situation was resolved. Taking control over our actions and thoughts is important but sometimes difficult to do. In order to control our total behavior, we have to first acknowledge that it is within our control.

---

**Thrive Thought:**

This chapter includes some really heavy psychological counseling theory material. I know this can be a lot to digest. You might be thinking, "Why do I need to know all this garbage?" This is so very important because it is the foundation of understanding how to be more effective in going after your goals. To point your car in the right direction and get to your destination in the quickest way possible, you have to know how to control the wheel. You have been swerving all over the road so far, and the rest of the chapters will help to give you steady control. Hang in there with me!

---

# CHAPTER 6

# What Day Is It?

We all have bad days, but most of us also have good days sprinkled in here and there. There are mornings when I wake up motivated. I know today is going to be a "triumph" day. It is a new day, and I am ready to take on the world with unmatched zeal. I will rise from bed early, get out and jog, eat healthy all day, be productive at work, and treat my family like royalty. When a crisis emerges during these days, I say, "Bring it on!" and face it head-on like some brave medieval knight slaying a fire-breathing dragon. I love those days!

Then there are the "neutral" days, which seem to happen more often than the other two. I wake up with no particular sense of motivation, but I get ready for work, maybe grab a breakfast shake, and head out of the door. On these days I typically do what is required of me at work and sometimes just a little more than that. I may watch what I eat here and there, but I give myself room to cheat because, hey, someone brought donuts. A crisis will emerge and I say, "I guess I should deal with this." I handle the crisis in the same way people handle something that comes across their desk at four forty-five on a Friday afternoon. I do what is necessary and little more. I come home and kiss my wife, play with my son a little, and am moderately productive. The day goes by as nothing really exciting, nothing new, and with not much learned.

Then there are the "other" days. Oh boy, the "other" days. These happen probably about as frequently as my "triumph" days, I am ashamed to say. I can tell when it is going to be an "other" day right from the start usually. Maybe I overslept, or maybe I went to brush my teeth and put some ointment cream on the toothbrush instead of toothpaste by accident (that really happened). Sometimes, on the "other" days, nothing particularly bad happens, but I am just in a foul mood. I do not want to see anybody, I do not want to talk to anybody, and I really, really, really want to go back to bed. These days I am terrible at work. I spend the majority of my time daydreaming, looking at Facebook, or researching the newest comic book movie rumors. Terrible, I know. On "other" days I am actively searching for comfort food, and it has to be within one hundred yards because I really do not want to move any farther than that. I leave a nice rear-end imprint on my chair at work because I have been plopped there almost all day, only moving to use the bathroom (it's less than one hundred yards from my desk). I tend to shirk responsibility, and my negative attitude is infectious. It seems that there is an atmosphere of pessimism created around me while I am in the midst of an "other" day. When there is a crisis, I go into the fetal position and hope that the situation resolves itself. I do not feel like doing anything, and I do not feel at all equipped to handle any sort of problem. When I get home on these "other" days, I tend to lack patience with my son. He can of course sense this with his super toddler powers and actively tries to push my buttons in every way imaginable (that's not true of course, but in my mind this is what is happening). On "other" days I am snippy with my wife and do not treat her with the love and respect she deserves. I go to bed having upset and angered the people who matter most to me, I have been so unproductive at work that it's embarrassing, and I have refused to grow or learn all day.

What is happening here? It seems as if I have described three completely different people! Am I losing my mind? Have I slipped into some sort of multiple personality situation? No, that's not it. If that were the case I think that just about the entire population would fall into that category. In fact, this kind of ebb and flow of different day-to-day personality characteristics is quite normal. However, you can take control over your total behavior and throw a big fat monkey wrench into this vicious cycle. I used to believe that these days were completely random and I had absolutely no control over which day came about when. I would wake up in the morning and basically just accept whatever day was handed to me.

However, if we take a closer look at the details in each day, we can examine the total behaviors taking place that either build momentum during a "triumph" day or continue the downward spiral of the "other" day. What is different in each day? On "triumph" days I wake up and am active. I get my shoes on and hit the pavement before the sun is even up. I have made a choice with my actions, and that choice has a strong influence over my total behavior. While outside jogging, I am activating my muscles, causing blood to flow and carry oxygen to my brain. Have you ever noticed that your mood can be greatly improved just by exercising? That is because exercise causes your body to experience a natural high: your brain is releasing chemicals that make you feel happy. This is why exercise is often part of recommended treatment for depression; it just makes you feel good. Having taken control over the action component of total behavior, I have already caused a change in my physiology. My physiology includes the release of chemicals that make me happy, and now my feelings have been positively affected. The final component of total behavior pretty much has no choice but to follow. My thoughts are innately positive at this point, as I am thinking thoughts such as, "This is awesome, bring on the day." On "triumph" days I am mindful of the food I eat and the liquids I drink, especially just after jogging. I choose the action of filling my body with healthy foods, usually full of protein, and my body reacts as a result. The protein helps me maintain my energy levels, and I am usually happy with myself for choosing the right foods. The components of total behavior are all working in my favor, and I feel as if I could take on the world.

On "neutral" days I wake up, usually at a decent time, and start my day by getting prepared for work. Sometimes I choose to eat healthy and sometimes not to eat healthy. I approach my day with indifference and wait to see what lies in wait for me. On these days the thoughts that course through my mind usually include "I really hope today is going to be a good day" or "Today might be a bad day." The resulting feeling is usually anxiety and uneasiness. On these days outside influences seem to easily sway me, and my interactions with others and my environment dictate my thoughts and feelings. The mornings are especially important on these days because the mornings seem to set the stage for the entire day. An argument with my wife can send me spiraling down but not usually as low as one of the "other" days. However, positive interactions lift me up, though not usually as high as "triumph" days. While it appears that outside influences are controlling my reactions and mood, the reality is that I am choosing to allow this to happen. If I take control of my actions and choose to remain positive in my interactions no matter what, my total behavior will follow and my day will improve greatly.

Now, let's talk about the dreaded "other" days. On these days I wake up in a foul mood, and things seem to go south from there. I feel sluggish; maybe I didn't sleep well. I know right when my day starts that it is going to be rough. Comfort food for breakfast, here I come. My interactions are inherently negative on these days, if I even speak to people at all. My thoughts typically include "I really don't like people," "Today is going to suck," and "Just let me get back in the bed." What effect are my choices having on my total behavior? My negative thoughts bring about negative emotions, and I usually try to compensate with comfort food. This food is of course *loaded* with sugar, which actually causes me to be more tired about half an hour later (physiology). This continues throughout the day as I do not want to move during the work day. My lack of motion brings about more negative thoughts, and, later in the day, I always have negative thoughts about having negative thoughts!

So now the question is, can my day shift from an "other" day in the beginning to a "triumph" day or is it set from the morning? Your day, your mood, and your outlook are always changeable. The reason that we seem to have entire days of pure joy or pure misery is that total behavior tends to create a snowball effect, a cycle of either positive or negative thoughts, actions, feelings/emotions, and physiology. Just remember that you are behind the steering wheel of the total behavior car. As the day goes on, that car picks up speed, but you can always grab the wheel and change directions. If you are going really fast, it can be difficult to make a quick turn without flipping the thing over, but a turn can be made. Just remember which wheels are in front. You have the most control over your actions and thoughts, with your actions being the easiest to manipulate. A favorite saying of Dr. Wubbolding's is that motion creates emotion. You probably need to be active the most when you least feel like moving. Create your own positive interactions, exercise, and be proactive with your goals.

This is a great recipe for daily success, but it is certainly no guarantee. There will still be days that are hard, and there will be days that are just plain bad. That is **OK** because it is a normal part of our human existence. Understanding and using the methods outlined later in this book do not guarantee instant and/or complete happiness. Instead, you will probably notice that you have more good days than bad and your bad days are not as bad as they used to be.

\* \* \* \*

Before we close out this chapter, I want to touch on some of the main criticisms of reality therapy.

Reality therapy and choice theory espouse that a person always has a choice, and for many this raises a red flag. "What about people who literally do not have a choice? What are they to do?" That is an excellent question and certainly a legitimate one. Even in situations where it seems like there is not a choice, there is. If someone holds a gun to your head and orders you to do something, you still have a choice. That choice may threaten your need for survival, but it is a choice nonetheless. Another criticism is "What about those with serious mental illness? Why would a person choose to be depressed or anxious? Doesn't reality therapy imply that the person chose this?" Yes and no. Just because reality therapy and choice theory say that there is always a choice does not mean that all the choices are healthy. Sometimes people are forced to choose between what is good and what is perceived as good. People always make the best choices they can given their knowledge, resources, and support system. Choices also reflect our best attempts to meet our basic human needs. We do not develop a pattern of behaviors that is not need-fulfilling; otherwise we would stop doing it on our own!

Whew! That is just the tip of the iceberg in regard to the concepts of reality therapy and choice theory, but it provides a solid foundation for moving forward with your goals. If you would like to learn more about reality therapy, I suggest reading *Reality Therapy for the 21ˢᵗ Century* by Robert Wubbolding.

---

**Thrive Thought:**

Having difficult days is part of the human existence. I do not want to mislead you; living a thrive life is not about being perfect or completely eradicating bad days. Eventually you will get to a place where you have more good days than bad, and you will notice that the bad days are not quite as bad as they used to be. Change begets change; small improvements will snowball and build momentum just like negative changes. Create some positive momentum today!

# PART II:

# Who Do You Want to Be?

It's time to start dreaming big! This portion of the book is likely where you will have the most fun—especially when you consider that the first part was probably as refreshing as a nice slap in the face! In the next several chapters, you will imagine what your best life is and learn strategies for narrowing down your goals. You will be encouraged to dream big while anchoring your dreams in reality. The next step after that is to map out the best route (creating objectives) to take you from where you are (Point A) to where you want to be (Point B, aka your goals). You have figured out where you are, and it is time to start looking toward where you are going and how to get there!

# CHAPTER 7

## Find Your Best You

What version of yourself is the best you? What do you want out of life? Every day you are becoming someone else. Even if you continuously have "neutral" days, you are always changing and becoming a new person. It is up to you whom that person ultimately will be. With careful attention and intentional total behavior, you can daily mold yourself into that person you want to be.

Before you can begin moving in a direction, you have to first decide which path to take, and this is no small task. Moving in a direction toward a particular goal will mean an investment of time and energy. This is a given, but it is imperative that you grasp this concept: whatever you choose to invest your time in is also a choice to not invest your time in other things. This sounds like a simple concept, but it was something that was lost on me for quite some time. In pursuing my degrees, I spent many hours sitting in a classroom and even more time working on assignments and studying for tests. For me this meant that I could devote less time to my family, church, other personal goals, and sleep. The path was not easy, but the sacrifice was well worth it because I viewed school as an investment. The time I was putting in would pay off later in the form of a need-satisfying profession, greater job stability, and a higher paycheck than I had ever earned in my life.

Think about the things in your life that are not an investment but more of a waste. For me these things were video games, watching television, and playing more video games. Please do not misunderstand me; I don't think video games are necessarily bad. I still play them, and they are wonderful stress relievers for me. The trick is that I don't devote nearly as much time to them. Remember that one of the basic human needs is fun, and I find video games fun. Just because something you do does not produce life-changing results does not mean you have to scrap the activity entirely; it may very well be need-fulfilling for you and very important. Just be cautious of how much time you are spending on these activities.

*A choice to invest your time in something is also a choice to not invest your time in something else.*

Hobbies are great; people need hobbies. The problem is when our hobbies, life goals, and purpose become unbalanced. This is why prioritizing your goals is so important.

Before we are able to get into the prioritizing of goals, we first have to define them. Your goals are yours and yours alone. The ultimate purpose for having goals and moving toward becoming a better person is to obtain need satisfaction. What is need-satisfying for me may not be for you and so on. For example, if you were to ask most people what they want out of life, you would hear an answer similar to "be happy and successful." These are great goals, but what in the world does that mean? Happiness and success are very abstract ideals and can be defined in a variety of ways. If you polled a hundred thousand people on what it means to be happy and successful, you would probably get many different answers. That is because, again, we all have different ways for satisfying our needs.

The CEO of a Fortune 500 company probably derives a sense of power and accomplishment from his or her career. Meanwhile, a janitor may experience the same amount of power satisfaction through his or her job. Is one person more happy or successful than another? What if I told you the CEO had been divorced four times and is not allowed to see his or her children? Perhaps the janitor is a retired military officer who just wants to keep busy. Whatever the case, people make their own happiness. There are many factors to consider here. Money does not define happiness or success, but a lack of money could certainly threaten our need for survival.

I am reminded of a quote from Viktor Frankl: "Don't aim at success. The more you aim at it and make it a target, the more you are going to miss it. For success, like happiness, cannot be pursued; it must ensue." What does this mean? If you shoot for a thrive life, *your* thrive life, success and happiness will follow and you will not have to chase them. Search inside yourself and ask, "What do I want from life?" Take a second to truly think about that question because this type of deep introspection is probably something you are not used to doing, but it is a great springboard for the solution-focused therapy you are about to use on yourself.

Solution-focused therapy is a relatively new theory in counseling/therapy and managed to turn the therapy world on its head. Solution-focused therapy is unlike any other form of therapy because the solution-focused therapist does not spend much time at all talking about your problems (crazy, right?). Instead, as the name implies, a solution-focused therapist is much more interested in what *is* working in your life. Look at the positives, look at when your problem is not a problem (there are almost always exceptions), and look at how you cope. There you will find your solution-focused therapy treatment. Take what works, replicate it, repeat. It's that simple.

There is a wonderful technique used in solution-focused therapy called the miracle question, and it is especially useful in helping people visualize their ultimate goals and determine what is most important to them. The miracle question is: **"Suppose tonight while you sleep, a miracle happens. When you awake tomorrow morning, what will you see yourself doing, thinking, or believing about yourself that will**

**tell you a miracle has happened in your life?"** This is not a question to take lightly, and I suggest that you write down the question and your answer. The answer to this question often reveals much of what we find need-satisfying, and the areas we need to work on for happiness to ensue. No one can tell you what your happiness is; go out and find it! Below are questions that will help you focus on the different domains in your life and get specific about what you want.

## Thrive Work:

Go ahead and grab a piece of paper or two and a pen. It's time to get to work! Read the questions below and answer each one on your sheet of paper. It would probably be best to brain-storm at first and just write down whatever comes into your mind. We will get more specific with our goals in a little bit.

What do you want for:
- Your family and the individual members of it?
- Your own personal growth?
- Your career?
- Your financial status?
- Your intellectual life?
- Your recreational time?
- Your spiritual development?

These categories cover nearly all aspects of your life, and they should each be considered very carefully. Similar to total behavior, all of these domains are interconnected and none is more important than another. However, just as we are all different, these different areas all represent different levels of need satisfaction for each of us. For example, some people find all of their need satisfaction in their family. This type of person feels a sense of love in being with his or her spouse and children; he or she feels power and accomplishment in being a good parent/spouse; he or she finds independence and freedom in raising children in the way he or she sees fit; he or she legitimately has fun spending time with family; and his or her need for survival is met though having a home and food on the table. If this is you, it is OK. Honestly speaking, this is not me. I derive a great sense of satisfaction in enhancing my intellectual life and my career. My sense of love and belonging comes from my family, but it is also OK to feel belonging from your coworkers. Even if you derive all of your need satisfaction from one area, it is still important to brainstorm and really meditate on these other areas of your life. It is entirely possible that you are not maximizing your need fulfillment.

**Thrive Thought:**

I love this chapter. It is so much fun to sit around and think of the ideal person we want to be. A lot of people do this sort of thing daily; I definitely did. I would dream of one day becoming this person who achieved great things, who made a genuine difference in this world, who could look himself in the mirror at night and go to bed happy. Prepare yourself because the next few chapters are all about work, but the work is necessary. If our goals never become anything more than random daydreams and thoughts, we are wasting our time. Have you imagined the best possible version of yourself? Good. It's time to start heading in that direction!

# CHAPTER 8

# What Does Your Thrive Life Look Like?

This chapter is where you will do the most work, so get ready. Remember that everyone's definition of success and happiness is different, and the challenge of this chapter is defining what *your* thrive life looks like. Your own goals may be similar to mine or someone else's, but they will likely not be the same.

Goal setting is something that most of us have been doing since grade school. I can remember learning about goals in elementary school and setting goals for myself in middle school. Of course these middle-school goals included things such as throwing a baseball seventy miles per hour, kissing a girl, and getting a Ken Griffey Junior rookie card. Looking back these goals can be considered somewhat silly, but they represented need satisfaction for me at the time. The problem with goal setting is that most of us have never learned how to do it right. Don't feel bad about that; goal setting is a skill, and a skill that no one is born knowing. You have to learn how to set goals and then practice them. Think of your life in terms of planning a trip. Before you can go anywhere, you first have to know where in the world you are. We covered that in a previous chapter, "Who Are You." Then, before we get moving in any direction, we have to discover exactly where we want to go. Setting goals is plotting a destination point, or points, for your life.

Have you made a brainstorm list from the previous questions? If not, go back and complete this exercise. This is the foundation for the rest of your goals and is absolutely essential. We are going to continue working with this list as we make our goals and get a clearer picture of who we want to be. I want you to narrow down your list to the top three for each category. We are going to refine this list, and one of the first things we need to do is cross off or change goals that are not directly within our control.

These are *your* goals; focus on what you can change and reasonably control. Too many times we tie our goals to other people or events that are outside of our control. When other people or events do not come through for us, we feel discouraged. When we do not reach these goals, we often say, "Forget it," and may quit goal setting all together. Don't set yourself up for failure! A goal of having a better marriage is phenomenal, but a marriage takes two. If your spouse is not as invested as you are, your marriage may not get better. In fact, it may get worse. A better example of a goal of this type is to be a better spouse. This goal puts the onus on yourself to do the work because you cannot be responsible for another person's actions. Even if your marriage does not improve, you have achieved your goal of becoming a better spouse.

Another example of a goal that is dependent upon others is getting a promotion at work. This is also a great goal, but it is certainly outside of your control. What if you are not qualified for the promotion position? Or what if someone else is just more qualified? An example of a goal that would be in your control is improving your performance at work. This goal puts control in your hands and allows you to say, "I am going to do the best I can, and that's all I can do." If other people are ultimately in charge of your goals being completed, you will likely find yourself frustrated and your goals unachieved.

## Thrive Work:

Cross off any brainstorm goals that you do not have total and complete control over, and narrow your list down to three goals for each category. It might look something like this (these are just examples and by no means have to be your goals).

- Your family and the individual members of it?
  - ❑ Spend more time with my family
  - ❑ Be a better father and husband
  - ❑ Get to know my in-laws better
- Your own personal growth?
  - ❑ Be healthier
  - ❑ Run a 10k
  - ❑ Lower my cholesterol

# What Does Your Thrive Life Look Like?

- Your career?
  - ☐ Find a job I enjoy doing
  - ☐ Improve my performance at work
  - ☐ Not have to work weekends
- Your financial status?
  - ☐ Be debt free
  - ☐ Begin a retirement account
  - ☐ Save a large amount of money
- Your intellectual life?
  - ☐ Read more books
  - ☐ Achieve a graduate degree
  - ☐ Do more brain-engaging activities (crossword puzzles, sudoku, etcetera)
- Your recreational time?
  - ☐ Get my yard in shape
  - ☐ Go on a vacation with my family
  - ☐ Join a sports league
- Your spiritual development?
  - ☐ Attend church regularly
  - ☐ Buy and use a daily devotional
  - ☐ Spend more time in prayer and meditation

There you go; we have goals! If your goals seem daunting and somewhat overwhelming, that's OK. They're goals, and you are not going to be there tomorrow.

Take a look at your list of goals; notice anything? There are a ton of them! This is an issue many of us don't consider when setting goals. If you tried to accomplish all of these goals at once you would probably burn out in a week. No, less than a week. Maybe even, like, half a day. Take a closer look at your goals; do a lot of them coincide with one another? In the previous example, one of my goals is to "find a job I enjoy doing." I also want to "achieve a graduate degree" for my intellectual life; these two can go hand-in-hand. By completing the goal of achieving a graduate degree, I would increase my options in career fields and improve my chances of finding a career I enjoy. Also, spending more time with my family would probably help me become a better husband and father or vice versa. And going on a vacation with my family would inherently mean spending more time with them. Don't tangle yourself up on goals that could produce the same results. We have a lot of goals—too many—and we need to simplify.

## Thrive Work:

Take a moment to examine your goals and then cross off the ones that could be accomplished by completing another goal. Once you have done this, go back through your remaining goals and number them by priority under each category. This might take some time. Don't worry if you have to take even a day or two to work through this step. You can put the book down to do some of this work. I won't be mad. It would be much more beneficial for you to truly take your time (remember, these are *your* goals) than to power through the whole book and skip the exercises.

# What Does Your Thrive Life Look Like?

It's time to think hard on your goals and determine "Which of these would mean the most for me to accomplish?" Your answer will come in the form of a prioritizing number next to each goal. Below is an example of what it might look like.

- Your family and the individual members of it?
  - ~~Spend more time with my family~~
  - Be a better father and husband (1)
  - Get to know my in-laws better (2)
- Your own personal growth?
  - Be healthier (1)
  - Run a 10k (2)
  - ~~Lower my cholesterol~~
- Your career?
  - ~~Find a job I enjoy doing~~
  - Improve my performance at work (1)
  - Not have to work weekends (2)
- Your financial status?
  - Be debt free (1)
  - Begin a retirement account (3)
  - Save a large amount of money (2)
- Your intellectual life?
  - Read more books (2)
  - Achieve a graduate degree (1)
  - ~~Do more brain-engaging activities (crossword puzzles, Sudoku, etc.)~~

- Your recreational time?
  - ◻ Get my yard in shape (1)
  - ◻ ~~Go on a vacation with my family~~
  - ◻ Join a sports league (2)
- Your spiritual development?
  - ◻ Attend church regularly (2)
  - ◻ Buy and use a daily devotional (3)
  - ◻ Spend more time in prayer and meditation (1)

OK, the process of elimination has begun and we are on our way to setting some goals! Chances are, though, you still have too many. In my example I still have sixteen! There is still work to be done. Let's keep chopping down those goals until we have a manageable amount.

I want you to know that the goals you are clearing out are not necessarily bad goals; they are just not what you want most right now. Do not feel as if you are giving up on these other goals or that you will never go for them again. They will still likely be there once you have accomplished what is most important to you.

## Thrive Work:

Go ahead and cross out any goal that is not number one under each heading. As you cross them out, make sure to write them down on a different piece of paper for later. Just because they are not your number one priority at this time does not mean they are bad goals! In fact, these may be great to keep around for your next round of goal setting after you have accomplished your first list. Your updated goal list should look something like this.

- Your family and the individual members of it?
  - ~~Spend more time with my family~~
  - Be a better father and husband (1)
  - ~~Get to know my in-laws better (2)~~
- Your own personal growth?
  - Be healthier (1)
  - ~~Run a 10k (2)~~
  - ~~Lower my cholesterol~~
- Your career?
  - ~~Find a job I enjoy doing~~
  - Improve my performance at work (1)
  - ~~Not have to work weekends (2)~~
- Your financial status?
  - Be debt free (1)
  - ~~Begin a retirement account (3)~~
  - ~~Save a large amount of money (2)~~
- Your intellectual life?
  - ~~Read more books (2)~~
  - Obtain a graduate degree (1)
  - ~~Do more brain-engaging activities (crossword puzzles, Sudoku, etc.)~~

- Your recreational time?
  - ☐ Get my yard in shape (1)
  - ☐ ~~Go on a vacation with my family~~
  - ☐ ~~Join a sports league (2)~~
- Your spiritual development?
  - ☐ ~~Attend church regularly (2)~~
  - ☐ ~~Buy and use a daily devotional (3)~~
  - ☐ Spend more time in prayer and meditation (1)

I know that this can be a painstaking process—making goals and then having to choose which ones you want the most—but it is necessary. This is where prioritizing really comes into play, and prioritizing is absolutely necessary to achieve your goals.

We are down to seven goals, which is fantastic, but I want you to prioritize these goals in a list. Priorities, priorities, priorities. Why does it matter what is most important to you? You are more likely to commit to goals you really want, things you truly want to go after. If you put down a goal you really don't care about, you are probably not going to accomplish it.

## Thrive Work:

Put what you consider to be your most important goal at number one, then number two, and so on. Your list will look something like this.

1. Be a better father and husband
2. Obtain a graduate degree

3. Be healthier
4. Be debt free
5. Spend more time in prayer and meditation
6. Improve my performance at work
7. Get my yard in shape

We are rolling now! You now have seven goals, and you have prioritized them one through seven! This is amazing progress and truly a gigantic leap toward becoming the person you want to be. We are not done with our goals yet, though. We have a ways to go, but if you made it this far you are doing great! It is time to ask some really tough questions about our goals and our motivations for them. Answer each of these questions for each of your goals.

• Is what I want attainable or realistic for me?
• Is there a reasonable chance of getting what I want in the near or distant future?
• How possible is it for me to make the changes in my own behavior that I've said I want to make?
• How would my life be different if I achieved my goals?

These questions will help you think critically about your goals and evaluate whether or not they are realistic. If you have not obtained a high school diploma, achieving a graduate degree is a great long-term goal, but a more realistic goal would be obtaining a diploma/GED and maybe even an associate's degree. If your goal, as in the example, is to be debt free and you have $100,000 in debt, this may not be a reality for you. While it is good financial practice to pay down and pay off debts, it is also true that there are some debts that most people live with. Also, if you have a goal of achieving a degree, you will have to consider that you may need student loans. Being debt free is a wonderful goal, but is it realistic for you? An example of an alternative and potentially realistic goal may be to pay off all credit card debt.

*If your goal is unrealistic or unattainable, just think about how frustrating it would be to continuously reach for it. It would be as if you were a little kid and someone much taller than you was dangling a candy bar just out of your reach. At some point you have to quit jumping up and down and go after a new candy bar!*

Speaking of candy bars, if you just completed those tasks you deserve one. Go ahead, it's OK to celebrate. If you truly just created seven goals that you really want to go after, it's time to congratulate yourself. Not one of those fake, pat yourself on the back deals. I mean, really, does anyone actually feel better after that? Do something you enjoy! You have really made tremendous progress, and do not sell yourself short. Change begets change and motion creates emotion; you are likely closer to the best you than you have ever been before!

## Thrive Thought:

If you are hoping to read through this book as fast as possible and find a magic remedy to make your life what you want it to be, just stop. It's not in here. I can't promise you "nine-minute abs" or "two weeks to a new you." What I offer you is the knowledge and skills to take control of your life like never before. It's time to stop taking shortcuts and get to work.

Now take a deep breath; that chapter was pretty intense. If you just went through the motions, reading that chapter just to get through it, go back and do some work. This is what it takes to make great changes! I know it's hard, but if it was easy, everyone would do it. Be exceptional!

# CHAPTER 9

# There Is No Try...

Now it is time to talk about commitment. You have created seven goals that you would like to achieve, and achieving these goals will mean you have become the person you want to be. But without commitment, these goals are just ideas on a piece of paper. Your level of commitment will be one of the biggest factors in determining whether or not you achieve your goals. Dr. Wubbolding believes that commitment exists at five levels. Let's take a look at these levels.

1. "I do not want to do this." This level of commitment is really no commitment at all. Since we brainstormed and worked very hard at narrowing down your goals, this is not likely a level that you will be on.

2. "I want the outcome, but I do not want to make the effort." This level of commitment is slightly higher than the first and acknowledges that the outcome is desirable. However, there is absolutely no commitment to action.

I believe we have all been at this level of commitment at different times in our life. Whenever diet commercials come on TV and the person who has allegedly dropped fifty pounds says, "I ate whatever I wanted and the pounds flew off!" I am a little tempted. It sounds great: the desired result but no work. But I am often reminded of the quote "Nothing worth having comes easy." This allows me to stop and realize that if I had everything I wanted with little to no effort, the things I wanted would not actually be that special.

3. "I'll try." This level of commitment indicates a willingness to change but has built-in excuses for failure. "I'll try" is often accompanied by other, similar ideas such as "I might," "I could," "maybe," and "probably." I am truly guilty of this phase of commitment, and this phase used to be my automatic go-to level for goals. I would tell myself, "I'll try to go to school and graduate." Then when it didn't work out (because of my own choices), I would look back and say, "Well, at least I tried!" Trying does not tend to elicit very much confidence. Imagine that you are on an airplane, and as you are nearing your destination, the pilot comes over the loudspeaker and says, "OK, folks, I am now going to try to land this plane." How would you feel at that moment? I think all of us expect more commitment than that, so why are we content with this level of commitment from ourselves? A great Jedi master once said, "There is no try. There is only do or do not."

4. "I will do my best." Now we are starting to get somewhere. In this statement we have an even higher level of commitment than the previous level, and we are seeing the beginnings of planning for action. However, there is still the escape clause of saying, "I tried my best, but it still did not work out." Saying you will try your best does not ensure 100 percent follow through.

5. "I will do whatever it takes." This is the highest level of commitment and usually is said by a person who has a specific plan for action. This person has evaluated all the possible outcomes and decided which path he or she is going to take no matter what. This person does not make excuses and instead makes intentional choices to bring him- or herself closer to completing his or her goals.

It is very important to note that goals can exist at different levels.

*It is impossible to go after all of your goals at the same time with a commitment level of five.*

The reason it is impossible is because there is just not enough time in the day to accomplish everything. That means you have to make choices—difficult ones. Remember, a choice to invest your time and energy into something is also a choice to not invest your time in something else. This means if your primary goal is to spend more time with your family, being in night classes and doing papers on the week-ends to earn a graduate degree will not move you toward that goal. You have to make choices, and now is the time to do it.

## Thrive Work:

Take a look at your seven goals again. Really, truly medi-tate on your commitment level to seeing each one through and then put that commitment in parenthesis beside each of your seven goals. It should look something like this.

1. Be a better father and husband (5)
2. Achieve a graduate degree (4)
3. Be healthier (4)
4. Be debt free (3)
5. Spend more time in prayer and meditation (3)
6. Improve my performance at work (3)
7. Get my yard in shape (2)

Since these are goals that you have brainstormed and really thought hard about, chances are that none of them will be at level one on the commitment scale. As you can see in the example, getting my yard in shape is a two on my commitment scale. That means that I want the outcome, but I don't really want to put in the work to see the results. Yeah, that sounds about right for yard work. If I made "get my yard in shape" as my primary goal, it would probably never be accomplished. Why? Because I am not very committed to that goal right now. Commitment levels can change over time, but right now that is not a goal I really want. I have three goals that are rated as a three on the commitment scale, two fours, and one that is a five.

Don't worry if you have a hard time with this; eliminating goals from your list should be somewhat difficult. Remember, these are all things you want to accomplish. However, we have to focus because seven is still way too many goals. Ultimately we should be down to three primary goals that we will create specific action plans for. Less than three is OK, but three needs to be the max.

I have said this before: as you remove goals from your list, do not throw them away. Be sure to put them on a separate paper so you can refer to them later. They are great goals, I'm sure, but they are just not your top priorities right now. Anything that has a commitment level below a three should probably be automatically taken off your list. If you left a goal on your list and your commitment level was "I want the outcome, but I don't want to work at it," how likely do you think it is that you will achieve that goal? Ideally, you will only have three goals that meet the criteria of being a four or a five on the commitment scale. If this is not the case, you will have to do some soul searching and choose three goals that you most want to achieve. This can be difficult, and so to help I advise using a balanced approach which will be outlined later.

**Thrive Thought:**

Commitment is a funny thing. It is an ideal that many people hold strongly, and we expect a certain commitment level from others. How often do we take a look at ourselves and really examine our commitment levels to our own goals? Probably not much...I know I never did. I would say, "Do I want to lose fifty pounds? Why yes, yes I do." And that was the end of it, as if saying, "Yes, I want this," was all the examining of commitment that needed to be done. These are goals that you want to achieve. Progress is progress; change begets change; motion creates emotion. Achieving goals creates momentum for yourself; don't rob yourself of that momentum by being too lazy to measure your commitment!

# CHAPTER 10

# Walk the Tight Rope

When it comes to living a thrive life, balance is an exceptionally important topic. Why is balance so important? Because you will fall over without it; literally and figuratively. The type of balance that I am describing is a mind/body/spirit balance. I know that even the phrase mind/body/spirit may elicit thoughts of Eastern religions and meditating on a mountain in Tibet with some goats. That's not exactly what I'm talking about. No plane ticket to Tibet is required for this. I am referring to taking responsibility for caring for the entirety of who you are.

## Body

Taking care of your body sounds simple. Eat right and exercise—duh. These are the basics of body care, but truly caring for your body goes well beyond those basic ideas. It is essential to have regular physicals and check-ups to make sure everything within your body is running properly. During one of these check-ups, you should consult with your physician on the exercise program and diet (if necessary) you plan on beginning. Getting out and exercising is great, but you must work up to high-intensity training or high weight activities. If you have never worked out a day in your life and you throw 250 pounds on a barbell to bench press, guess what? It's probably going into your face; that's not fun.

Know your limits and remember to stretch. Stretching is so important for your muscles, even if you just plan on going for a long walk. Failure to stretch properly can result in numerous injuries that could keep you sidelined for a while.

Don't forget the simple things. If you are going to be outside for a long time, be sure to apply the appropriate sunscreen to keep your skin safe. Be mindful of the different vitamins you can take to maximize your body's performance as well.

## Mind

Your mind works in a way that is similar to your body. The only way for your muscles to grow is if you challenge them. You have to make them work so they can break and be rebuilt. This is what happens when you lift weights; the muscles snap and are rebuilt stronger. Your mind is at its healthiest when it is being challenged. Easy ways to keep your mind sharp include doing crossword puzzles, sudoku, or other mentally stimulating activities. Also, learning a new skill requires that you stretch your mind a little. Have you ever wanted to learn to play an instrument? This is a great way to grow your mind in new ways and keep your brain sharp and healthy.

Another interesting study of the mind is neuroplasticity. In his book *Pocket Guide to Interpersonal Neurobiology*, Daniel Siegel describes this very topic as well as many others related to the mind. Neuroplasticity is defined as the ability of the mind to change its structure in response to experience. So much of our lives are spent not paying attention to who we are and what is going on in the moment that we go on "autopilot" (more on this topic in a later chapter). By taking charge, being intentional, and focusing specific attention through mindfulness in integrative ways, a person can actually change the structure of his or her brain! This is not something that a person can learn about one night, put into practice, and expect a change the next morning. This has to be practiced, and it has to be practiced a lot. Dr. Siegel describes seven, possibly eight, aspects of our lives that support neuroplasticity. In reading this list, you will see connections between our bodies, relationships with others, and our minds.

1.  Aerobic exercise: reasonable, voluntary exercise is so beneficial in so many ways. Here is just one of them. Exercise supports continued brain growth.
2.  Good sleep: sleep is most effective and refreshing when we reach the stage of sleep known as rapid eye movement (REM) stage. That is why the term *good sleep* is used instead of just sleep.

3. Good nutrition: in order for the brain to function properly, it has to be properly nourished.
4. Relationships: our relationships with others.
5. Novelty: exposing the brain to new stimuli (learning a new skill, experiencing a new culture, etcetera) is important for growing the brain.
6. The close paying of attention: by focusing on a specific task or moment instead of going on "autopilot" or multitasking, we can stimulate the release of chemicals that support neuroplasticity.
7. Time-in: this is where mindfulness comes into play. By taking specific time to focus inwardly on our feelings, thoughts, and state of being, we encourage the growth and integration of neural circuits.
8. Humor (maybe): some preliminary studies have shown that healthy growth of the brain is promoted through laughter.

## Spirit

You might be thinking, "OK, body I get, and mind makes sense, but how do I take care of my spirit?" Great question. Your spiritual self is engaged through your connection with the world, others, and, of course, spirituality. If you do not consider yourself to be a "spiritual" person, that is OK. Your spirit, as I refer to it, covers so much more than just religion or believing in a higher power. Years ago, I was overly focused on the religious aspect of myself. I was so consumed with the religious aspect that I forgot another key component of my spiritual self: my relationships with others. I forsook my relationships with others to achieve what I believed to be some sort of transcendental religious state, but in actuality I was just a misguided individual who was far unhealthier than he realized. I let my body go to the point of obesity, and my mind was dull as could be. I completely mistook my spiritual side as only being represented by religion.

We are social creatures, and the relational aspect of our lives cannot be overstated. From birth nearly everything we do in life has some sort of social context to it. Stop for a moment and think about all your current problems. How many of them have to do with other people? It is likely that most of your issues have something to do with others; it's just part of the human experience. It is important to understand our roles in these issues, cultivate positive social skills, and try our best to maintain healthy relationships. Just as most of our issues have something to do with others, most of our triumphs are socially related as well. Think of all your greatest moments; how many of them have to do with other people? As we move along in executing your objectives and ultimately your goals, your support system will be absolutely vital.

Since your mind, body, and spirit all reside within you, they are inseparable. In seeking to improve one aspect of your functioning, you will usually find that there are benefits to be had in the other areas as well. For example, if you are improving your mind by attending courses at the local college, you will likely be in class with others and potentially improving your connectedness to others and therefore your spiritual self. If you start jogging, you may notice that you can think more clearly while running. This is likely because you are taking in more oxygen and experiencing greater blood flow, which helps to "clear your mind."

Remember: balance and moderation. Becoming overly concerned with improving only one aspect of your functioning can lead to an out of balance life and an unhappy person. It is of course possible to be more focused on one aspect and is in fact a state in which most of us live. Improving one area of mind, body, or spirit does not necessarily mean that you are living to the exclusion of other areas. Just remember to feed all three as often as possible!

## Thrive Work:

Back to our goals. We are in the process of narrowing down our goals to only three. I suggest, again, selecting one that will focus on improving your mind, one for your body, and one for your spirit (relationships, spirituality, etcetera). Your fantastic list of three amazing goals may look something like this.

1. Be a better father and husband
2. Achieve a graduate degree
3. Be healthier

Yes! We have completed our list of goals. Step back, take a deep breath, and enjoy this moment. This is a *huge* step toward becoming the person you want to be. OK...whew...back to work!

You will notice something about your goals. They sound awesome, but how do you get there? In most cases our goals consist of abstract ideas and need a way to bring some concreteness to them. What does being a better father and husband look like? How will you know when you have achieved your goals? Your goals are great, but they are just words. They will continue to be just words until you create and enact an action plan. Your action plan is going to include breaking down your goals into very specific objectives.

---

### Thrive Thought:

You should now have three goals. Three goals! These aren't just any three goals though. You have done some deep introspection and asked yourself some very tough questions. These are *the* three goals. This is big and you should really be proud of yourself. So far you have laid out exactly where you are and exactly where you want to go. In the next chapter, we will plot out specific points that will lead you from where you are to where you want to be.

---

# CHAPTER 11

# Thrive Points

Living a thrive life is your ultimate goal, but that's not going to happen all at once (that would be nice though, right?). So how do you get from where you are to where you want to be? Let's take a second to break it down. Making an entire lifestyle shift is daunting—a task that is so difficult you might think, "Why even try?" You should try because you *can* do this; you just haven't been taught the skills yet. You *can* change your life, and you will—it just won't happen all at once. Big changes are most effectively accomplished through small and specific changes: thrive points. Think of thrive points as objectives or tasks to help you accomplish your goals. You are currently at point A, and your goals are at point B. The objectives are the path you will travel to get you where you want to go. We have three goals! Yay! That is certainly something you should be proud of, but these great goals will just be words on paper unless you create a plan.

Objectives should always be three things: specific, achievable, and measurable (SPAM!). Do not be afraid to get really specific with your objectives. If one of your objectives for becoming a better husband and father is to spend more time with your family, how much time? Every night? Three nights a week? Maybe five? If an objective is to go on more family outings, how many? Being specific gives you direct guidelines for how to complete your objectives and ultimately achieve your goals. How will you know whether or not you are making progress unless you have something you can measure? This sounds like such an obvious question, but it is something we often overlook when setting goals for ourselves. We are talking about really long-term goals in a lot of circumstances, and failing to set up ways to measure our progress can make achieving our goals feel like a task we can never complete. Due to this, we will give up a lot of times, even when we were making progress!

Your objectives should also be achievable. Setting an objective of being able to jog fifteen miles by next week or spending six hours a day playing with your kids is great but probably not achievable. Do not be afraid to stretch yourself and reach new heights but also be able to recognize when that candy bar is just too high! You can create as many objectives as you want for your goals, but you usually want to have at least five per goal. And remember: SPAM (SPecific, Achievable, and Measurable).

## Thrive Work:

Go ahead and write down some objectives under your three goals. Here are some examples.

1. Be a better father and husband
   a. Spend two hours a night playing with my children at least four nights a week for the next six months
   b. Go on a date night with my wife (just the two of us) three nights a month for the next six months
   c. Go on one family vacation over the next six months that lasts at least three days
   d. Attend at least 80 percent (four out of five) of my children's sporting events/school functions over the next six months
   e. Prepare dinners at home at least four nights a week for the next six months
2. Achieve a graduate degree
   a. Register for and take the GRE (Graduate Record Examination) within the next three months
   b. Of the classes I register for, attend at least 90 percent of the class meetings
   c. Spend at least one hour a night, four nights a week studying or completing assignments
   d. Complete all assignments at least three days before they are due
   e. Apply for at least three scholarships

3.  Be healthier
    a.  Calculate my basal metabolic rate to determine how many calories I should be taking in daily by the end of this week
    b.  Research at-home exercise programs (P90x, INSANITY, etcetera), make a decision, and purchase one by the end of next week
    c.  Begin walking five days a week for half an hour, either before or after work
    d.  Educate myself by reading at least two books about nutrition and physical health within the next six months
    e.  Schedule a physical within the next month

As you can see, when you start putting objectives below your goals, you realize how quickly your time becomes committed. In just the example above I have committed myself to spending two hours a night at least four nights a week playing with my children, going on a date night with my wife three nights out of the month, spending one hour a night at least four nights a week studying, and walking for half an hour five days a week. I am suddenly a very busy person. If I want to achieve my objectives and thereby achieve my goals, I have to be both organized and dedicated to the outcome. You can probably see now why having more than three simultaneous goals could be tricky. Usually, if you are striving for more than three goals at a time, you are going to fall short of at least one just because there is not enough time in the day.

**Thrive Thought:**

When working with a client in therapy, the therapist must create what is called a treatment plan. The treatment plan is a document created by the therapist and client that states what the client wants to work on, how he or she is going to work on these things, and when he or she wants to accomplish these goals. Guess what, friend? You are basically working on your own treatment plan. No, this doesn't mean you need a therapist. Treatment plans are really effective (why else would we do it?) and are great for helping both the therapist and the client focus. Feeling focused? You should be. Thrive on!

# CHAPTER 12

# Baby Steps Are Still Steps

These goals and objectives represent a lot of work. This is not something that should be taken lightly or jumped into recklessly. Three goals should be the *maximum* at any one time because more than three just takes too much time. It is OK to only have one or two goals, especially if you lead a very busy life. It would be hard to achieve several goals and objectives if you have an overly demanding job, several children, church commitments, and any other number of commitments. Do not feel as if you have to have three goals in order to become a better version of yourself. Change begets change. This means that small changes, even though they may seem insignificant, can have a huge impact on future functioning and lead to greater changes down the line. Making small changes that are barely noticeable is not fun. Writing down big goals for doing great things—that's fun!

Have you ever tried to change too much too fast? I was the king of this. I would lie awake at night and decide that, starting the next morning, my new routine would be waking up at four in the morning, jogging for two miles, and then coming back to the house and lifting weights. Oh yeah, and starting that next morning I was also going to cut carbs and sweets out of my diet completely, read more books, and start taking classes at the college. Guess how far I made it with those goals? All the way to the snooze button. It usually worked for about a day or so, but it was too much too fast. Not only that, but when I crashed off a diet, I crashed hard, usually into Doritos - with my face. My goals were so lofty, and I felt so terrible for not reaching them that I would spend two days on the couch eating sweets because I felt guilty. And then I felt guilty for that! My health was in worse shape than when I began setting goals in the first place.

The point is that you have to be realistic with these goals and work toward something you can actually accomplish. For some people, losing five pounds is a fantastic goal; reading one book is a great goal; introducing yourself to one new person a week is a great goal. These do not seem like life-changing goals, but progress is progress; change begets change; motion creates emotion. Want to feel better about your goals? Achieve them. Don't be afraid of baby steps. If you are moving toward your goal, you are closer than where you were yesterday. If you keep taking those baby steps, you will eventually get to where you want to be.

If you made it through this section and completed your goals and objectives, you have done a lot. Determining the person you want to be takes some serious effort and soul searching. Many times in life we do not put forth the thought and planning necessary to carry out and complete our goals, and then we wonder why we fall short. You have the power and the choices to bring about wonderful changes in your life that are need-satisfying and can bring you closer to your own happiness. Now you know where you are (chapter 1, "Who Am I") and what your destination is (goals), and you have a map to get there (objectives). All you have to do now is steer your total behavior car down the path.

---

**Thrive Thought:**

This chapter was really hard for me to grasp (it still is). I am a recovering pessimist and cynic—basically a glass half-empty guy. This is a terrible mind-set when working on goals. Why? Anything short of the goal is failure. Even if I accomplished my goals, I used to have excuses for why it wasn't done right (I do better now). Remember that every day you are moving in one direction or another. If you are able to take hold of that movement and direct it toward your goal, it does not matter how little you have moved. The point is that you are closer to your goal!

---

# PART III:

## The Journey

We have thus far discovered who you are (point A), who you want to be (point B, goals), and how you plan to get there (your objectives, mapping your steps). Those are monstrously huge steps toward becoming the best version of you, but we still have to talk about the journey. The journey is the most difficult part because this is where all the hard day-to-day work actually comes in. Sure, it was difficult to visualize where you are now, conceptualize goals, and agonize over achievable objectives, but this is where you wake up in the morning and say, "Bring it on!" The most important thing to remember is that every single day, every single moment you have a choice. Your choices are shaping the person you are becoming. The question is not whether you are capable of achieving your goals or not (you are); the question is whether or not you have the skills and mind-set to follow through. In the next few chapters there are several different strategies and tools for helping you achieve your goals.

# CHAPTER 13

# Reframe!

OK, so you already know that I am an admitted recovering pessimist and cynic. Because of this, I have had to seriously practice changing my mind-set...especially when it comes to my goals. Why does it matter? Progress is as much a state of mind as it is an actual measurable change. This is an idea that cannot be stressed enough. Staying positive does not just involve closing your eyes and thinking happy thoughts, praying they're happy enough to get you off the ground and flying around with the rest of Neverland. Staying positive involves changing the way you think, talk, and behave.

Reframing is a tool that is taught to first-year counseling students, and it is practiced throughout their education. Why? Because it is something people need; it is very helpful. With the right mind-set, language, and behaviors, nearly any situation can be viewed through a positive light. Did you fail to reach your goals? Nope—you learned what not to do next time. Only dropped two pounds instead of fifty? You still lost weight. Did you fail that class you registered for? That's OK; you learned that you may need a tutor for that subject. Stay positive! Positivity is contagious and creates positive momentum in your life. Change begets change, progress is progress, and motion creates emotion. (You are probably tired of reading this, but you have got to grasp it.)

Too often when we think about changing, setting goals, and becoming a new person, we tend to focus on the negative aspects of our life that we want to change. Duh. If it wasn't negative, we wouldn't want to change it. I am going to challenge you on this though. It's time to get away from the language of problems (what most of us speak) and focus on the language of solutions (here comes some more solution-focused therapy). I want you to really think about positive and negative speech. Have you ever been around a person who was just negative all the time? His or her negativity feels contagious and seems to infect the atmosphere around him or her. Negativity is a stink that no shower can clean off, and it will pull you down if you let it.

Think again about your problems and the things you want to change in your life; you automatically had negative thoughts, right? That's completely normal, but it's time to change your perspective. Usually when we engage in "problem talk," we are speaking in the negative, focusing on the past, and implying permanency in our problems.

OK, now think about that person you know who is nothing but positive all the time. For a recovering pessimist and cynic like me, these people can be annoying sometimes. They are just *so* positive all the time and so happy. I noticed something else about them as well: they have a lot of people who want to be close to them. Everyone seems to want to be their friend (including me). Why is that? Positivity is just as contagious as negativity. A positive disposition spreads like the flu, and suddenly just by being around that positive person, you are a little happier. Do you think those kinds of people are just naturally positive? Maybe. Odds are though that they had to practice having a positive mind-set until it became second nature. I know this can be difficult to do, but start practicing and eventually you will automatically begin thinking and saying positives. Take it from a recovering pessimist.

When it comes to our perspective, we make our issues bigger than they are, and in our mind they eventually become insurmountable. The language of solutions is positive, helpful, and future-oriented. Remember, the future is ever-changing and is being decided by the choices you make today. Instead of seeing your problem as "a problem," see it as an opportunity. You have the chance to take the challenges in your life and turn them into your triumphs. This is reframing.

Language is so important, but it becomes automatic for us. If we constantly speak negatively (I used to), you might not even notice when you do it. When speaking about your "problem," try to use the past tense. Using words such as "were" and "have been" will help keep you focused on the possibility of change. Demonstrate an expectation for change by using words such as "yet" or "when" instead of "if" or "would." Instead of "If I achieve my goals" say, "When I achieve my goals." Instead of "I cannot pass this class" say, "I have not been able to pass this class yet," or, "When I pass this class." It may seem silly, but our language has a direct connection to our thoughts (more on that in a bit). Making simple changes in the way we speak, especially to ourselves, can have far-reaching implications with our expectations for change.

## Thrive Work:

In regard to thinking positively, pull out your goals again. Uh-oh. You probably thought we were done editing them. Almost, I promise. Your goals should be framed in positive terms instead of negative ones. You may be thinking, "They're goals! Of course they're positive!" And you are right in a sense. Any goal that represents a decrease in behavior is a negative goal. For example, "To lose weight" or "Stop fighting with my spouse" are examples of negative goals. Positive goals would be "To become healthier" or "To increase my positive interactions with my spouse." Focus on the gain and not the loss. Why is this important? It is the difference between the language of problems and the language of solutions.

Examples of negative goals:
- To lose weight
- To stop skipping school
- To quit getting into arguments with my kids

Examples of positive goals:
- To become more healthy
- To attend school more frequently
- To have a healthier relationship with my kids

OK. Now we have begun using solution-focused language to change the way we talk to each other and ourselves about our goals. We have spent so much time thus far talking about and thinking about our problems, it is time to think about our strengths. We all have unique and powerful ways of dealing with situations in our lives, and you will need to call on your strengths to complete your goals. Just thinking about your strengths and what you are good at is not good enough; we are going to write them down (more solution-focused therapy).

## Thrive Work:

I want to challenge you right now to write down five of your strengths that will help you complete your goals. This may actually be difficult for some people because those of us who are recovering pessimists do not think about our strengths much. This is part of changing your speech and thoughts to the language of solutions. It may take some time, but when your strengths come to you, be sure to write them down on the same paper that you wrote your goals on. Your strengths should be your own and should be things that will help you achieve your goals. Be sure to use "I" statements;

own your strengths! Here is an example of what this may look like.

1. I have good organization skills.
2. I possess great communication skills.
3. I have good insight into my problem areas and a plan for change.
4. I have above-average determination.
5. I am disciplined enough to follow through with my objectives.

Having strengths is great, but they are useless unless you know what they are and how to use them. Pull out your goals, think about which strengths will help with which goals, and put the goal number next to your strength. Trust me, you have more skills and strengths than you realize. You are just not used to identifying and using them. Here is an example.

1. I have good organization skills. **(2, 3)**
2. I possess great communication skills. **(1, 2)**
3. I have good insight into my problem areas and a plan for change. **(1, 2, 3)**
4. I have above-average determination. **(1, 2, 3)**
5. I am disciplined enough to follow through with my objectives. **(1, 2, 3)**

## Thrive Thought:

This chapter may seem a little gimmicky, and you are probably thinking, "Come on, what's the difference if my goal says 'lose weight' or 'gain health'?" These are the small things that increase your chances of success. Give yourself the greatest opportunity for success; stay positive! As a side note, consciously changing the way you speak to the language of solutions will eventually cause this to be automatic. Remember that incredibly positive person whom everyone wants to be around? That could be you before you know it.

# CHAPTER 14

# Be Mindful

Before we speak about being mindful, let's talk a little bit about the opposite: mindlessness. Have you ever got in your car to drive somewhere, arrived at your destination, and got out of your car thinking, "I don't remember anything about that drive!" Or maybe you picked up a candy bar and the next thing you know, you are left holding an empty wrapper. These are just a couple of examples of mindlessness. Mindlessness is when, for lack of a better phrase, our mind goes on autopilot. Mindlessness is one of the most terrible afflictions you can have when trying to reach your goals. As a society, we have become fully consumed with multitasking and ensuring that everything we do is as fast and efficient as possible. This mind-set has cultivated a society of people (myself included) who tend to go on autopilot a lot. Mindfulness involves being consciously aware of ourselves and our surroundings at any given moment. It is being aware of oneself on purpose.

# Be Mindful

Being aware of our total behavior—thoughts, feelings, physiology, and actions—is especially useful when monitoring one's own thoughts and speech for negative talk. Mindfulness alone will not eliminate our problems, but through mindfulness we can gain more control over our total behavior by being more aware of the things we have been "automatically" doing. Do you remember our total behavior car? Actions and thoughts make up the front two wheels while feelings and physiology are the rear wheels. How can you control your total behavior if you are not even aware of it? Mindfulness allows us to be aware of where we are steering the car. Pay attention; no autopilot!

As with any new skill, mindfulness takes practice. This is not something you can just decide to do and do it right now with no problems, especially because we have conditioned ourselves for mindlessness. It can be easy to confuse mindfulness with concentration, and as we discuss mindfulness, you will find that the two are certainly connected. As you go through the exercises that follow, you will probably notice that your concentration improves as well.

There are certainly similarities between the mindfulness and concentration, but the differences are worth noting. Concentration is simply focusing attention on something and is a very important skill. Being able to concentrate on and complete tasks is necessary to be productive. Mindfulness, however, goes a step beyond concentration. Mindfulness involves a presence of mind. Still not making sense? That's OK, because we are going to go through some mindfulness exercises together.

1. Just one minute: this exercise is easy and can be done at any time during the day. I suggest that you try to do this right now. Find a quiet place with little to no distractions or sounds. Check the time on your watch or phone, and for the next sixty seconds, focus all of your attention on your breathing. Even though this only lasts for one minute, it may feel like much longer. You can leave your eyes open and do not change your breathing rate. Your mind will likely wander, but that is OK. You have to train your mind to be able to focus because all of us have been training ourselves for mindlessness. If you can't maintain your concentration on your breathing for a full minute, that is OK. You have to start somewhere, so keep trying! You should attempt this exercise several times throughout the day and at least three times a day to help with focus and clarity. You may find that over time a minute becomes no challenge at all. In that case feel free to try to extend your concentration even further.

2. Mindful observation: this exercise involves picking up an object you have laying around—really, any object is fine. It could be a pencil, paper clip, cup, etcetera. Hold the object in your hands and allow your

attention to be completely focused on the object. Do not assess or think about the object, just observe it. This is another exercise that takes time and practice, but over time you may feel a renewed sense of "being present" or "being awake." Over time your mind will release thoughts of past or future, and you will be in the moment. Be aware of this feeling and how different it is from your normal state of mind. Notice the current time and try to focus for three minutes. Just like the other exercises, as you become better at conscious observation, try to extend the amount of time you are able to hold your concentration.

3. Cues: this exercise is a little more advanced. As you find yourself becoming more adept at completing the first two exercises, you may want to attempt this one. This exercise involves you focusing your attention on your breathing whenever you hear a specific environmental cue. One example would be to focus on your breathing every time you hear the phone ring. Choosing your cue is very important. You do not want to choose one that you will hear five thousand times a day. For example, if you work in an office, you probably do not want to use the clicking of a mouse. Also, you do not want to choose a cue that you will never hear either. If hearing a lion's roar is your cue, it's probably not going to happen. Find something that works for you. Some people's cues include: every time

they look in the mirror, every time they wash their hands, every time they touch their hair, etcetera.

4. Listening to music: did you know that there is an actual type of therapy called music therapy? Music therapy is evidence-based and helps individuals accomplish goals utilizing music interventions. Pretty cool, huh? Have you ever been listening to a song, a great song, and when it was over, you realized that you completely lost track of time, where you were, etcetera? Music has wonderful therapeutic properties and can provide a sense of escapism. Just listening to music is great, but I am going to ask you to take it a step further. Turn on some music, preferably something that has a somewhat slow tempo and is soothing. As the music plays, focus on the sound and vibration of each note and pay attention to the feelings that the music brings about within you as well as any other sensations you feel. You may find that other thoughts creep into your head during this time. That's OK. Just notice them and bring your attention back to the music.

5. Cleaning the house: yes, this is an actual mindfulness exercise and not some trick to get someone to clean up a little! The name "cleaning house" has a double meaning in this instance. It literally means cleaning your house but also figuratively means getting rid of your emotional baggage. Have you ever

felt incredibly stressed out while sitting at home and come to the realization that "my place is so dirty that it makes me stressed!" This is fairly common, as clutter (in our homes and within us) can be a strong source of stress and anxiety. Because of this, decluttering or the act of cleaning up can be very therapeutic and used as a mindfulness technique. In order to get the full effect of being mindful, you first have to change your perspective on cleaning. Do not think of it as a chore or a job but rather think of it as a positive event or a stress-relieving activity. You can combine music with this exercise to bring about even more of a positive effect. As you are cleaning, don't just mindlessly allow your thoughts to wander; truly focus on what you are doing. Notice the warm and soapy water on your hands as you wash dishes; feel the vibrations of the vacuum cleaner as you clean the floors; notice the textures and warmth of the laundry as you fold it. This may sound somewhat strange to you, but give it a shot. You may be surprised at just how therapeutic cleaning house can be when you change your perception and become mindful.

6. Time-in: you are probably aware of what time-out is, especially if you have kids. If you don't know, time-out is that thing that parents continually threaten children with because they would feel bad if they spanked them all the time (I'm guilty too). Time-out

basically means taking a break or being removed from an activity or situation for some time. Relating it to sports, time-out means that the game stops for a moment and everyone has a chance to catch his or her breath. Let's talk about time-in. Time-in is where you intentionally take time to disconnect, be alone, and look inward. Time-in is very similar to what a lot of people would call prayer or meditation. Being alone, quiet, and observant of your thoughts and feelings are essential to time-in. You don't have to spend hours upon hours with time-in; just start with five minutes a day. You are training yourself to take control and shut off the autopilot mode.

Remember that mindfulness is a skill, and like learning any new skill, it takes practice. Warning: you will not be good at this right away, and you may even not like doing it. I am asking you to trust me and stick with it though. As you go through these exercises, you will probably find that your ability to concentrate and focus improves as well as your ability to be mindful at will. We are programmed for mindlessness, so accomplishing these tasks may be more difficult than you think. You are rewiring your brain, so give yourself time. Switching from autopilot to awareness can be a tough road. It is OK to struggle at first, and you will get better at mindfulness as you keep up the practice. Do not feel as if you have to wake up tomorrow and engage in all five exercises right away for hours a day. I would suggest starting with the first exercise because it is the simplest to accomplish and takes very little time. As you progress, feel free to try out the other ones. If there is an exercise that you do not particularly like, then do not do it. These exercises are geared toward helping you become more mindful and present with yourself, and you should make them your own.

## Thrive Thought:

Mindfulness will be very useful in helping you achieve your goals, but there are other benefits to being more mindful. Research suggests that the act of mindfulness, or conscious awareness, is one of the keys to neuroplasticity. Neuroplasticity is the ability of the human brain to rewire, grow, and develop. This is very important for keeping your mind sharp but also in maintaining and improving your ability to learn throughout your life. This is good stuff!

# CHAPTER 15

# Control Your Musturbation Habits

We all do it, and it's OK to admit. Heck, most of us do it several times a day. I am willing to bet, however, most people don't even realize that they are doing it. It started innocently enough when they were young, and now it is nothing more than a habit. Musturbation is bad for your health and can have a serious impact on your psychological well-being.

All right, slow down and get your mind out of the gutter. I am not talking about what you think I am talking about. Musturbation is one of the more common types of cognitive distortions. I know what you are thinking now: "What the heck is a cognitive distortion?" A cognitive distortion is a thought that is irrational or not based on fact.

Musturbation is a term coined by Albert Ellis to describe what a person does when he or she is stuck in whether or not he or she "must" do something. For example, "I *must* have dinner ready every evening by six." This may seem a little extreme to some people, but it's an example of something that is very real in our lives. We all have "musts" that we bring with us from our upbringing and past experiences. Musturbation has to be dealt with because it leads to rigid thinking and unfair evaluations of ourselves or others based on whether or not our silly "must" is met.

What does musturbation have to do with your goals? Everything. I cannot remind you of total behavior enough. Our thoughts, actions, feelings, and physiology are all connected. Allowing cognitive distortions to be in your life will negatively impact your thoughts. Negative thoughts lead to negative emotions, negative behaviors, and a physiological response...the cycle goes on. So, what should you do? Replace your irrational thoughts with rational ones. Easy peezy, right? Opposite! This is another skill you will have to practice, and it will take some time, but you can do this. Relax a little because I am going to help you learn the skills to overcome irrational thinking.

Judging our thoughts as rational or irrational and replacing unhealthy thoughts with healthy ones is the goal. That is putting the cart a little bit before the horse though. Before we can judge and replace thoughts, we must first learn how to observe them. Our thoughts are especially important to pay attention to because our thoughts and actions are the components of total behavior most within our control. Taking control over your thoughts is one of the two quickest ways to effective change.

If we want to control our thoughts, we must first learn how to listen to them. Thoughts are another part of our life that we tend to put on autopilot and not even notice. Oftentimes they are just automatic and whish through our brains without a second glance. We have thousands upon thousands of thoughts each and every day, most of which go unnoticed. If our thoughts are distorted or out of touch with reality in some way, how likely is it that our perception is also out of line?

Think about the last time you were at the beach or a pool, having a good time and enjoying yourself as well as the people with you. The next thing you know, someone walks out who is in phenomenal shape. He or she is probably some sort of triathlete—forget that, a quadathlete. I mean, you could break a sledgehammer over his or her abs. What thoughts are going through your mind? Don't be ashamed because it is human nature to have these thoughts. I immediately think, "Boy I'm fat!" and reach for a towel or my shirt to cover up. Whether I am actually fat or not, the thought is there. Over in the corner of the pool area, you see a couple of people laughing, and you automatically think, "They are laughing at me. They see how fat I am and they are laughing." Where does this type of thinking lead? Perhaps the people were laughing at a joke they were sharing. Sure, it is entirely possible that they were laughing at you, but is it probable? Even if they were laughing at you, would it matter?

# Control Your Musturbation Habits

This is why being mindful of our thoughts it so important. It is absolutely human nature and automatic to go down roads that lead to self-loathing, distorted perceptions, negative thoughts, and ultimately an inability to reach our goals. My thoughts went to a negative place, and the rest of my total behavior has no choice but to follow. My thought "Boy I'm fat!" leads to emotions including shame, embarrassment, and self-loathing. My body is telling me that I am now hungry for sugar because this makes me feel better about myself, and my actions are following right along. Before I know it, one simple cognitive distortion has torpedoed my afternoon.

Just like the other mindfulness techniques, you will have to practice observing your thoughts. *You will not be good at this right away.* Try to find a quiet place and focus on your thoughts. Do not attempt to analyze your thoughts at this point; just notice them. Do not be judgmental (yet) and do not try to counter your thoughts. Just pay really close attention to them. Be aware of what they are.

As you progress in your ability to notice your thoughts, you will be ready to take the next step: journaling. I know that journaling is something that can be tedious and not very much fun, but the rewards are well worth the sacrifice. I suggest that you find a journal that is small enough to take with you, and when you practice observing your thoughts, begin to write them down along with the date. You do not need a long narrative or detailed descriptions about the environment. "It was a dark and cloudy morning. I awoke with a stir as I noticed my alarm was buzzing slightly different than usual. My eyes did not want to open, and my body begged me to stay in bed. 'I'm tired,' I thought to myself." All right, slow down with that stuff, James Patterson. None of that is helpful. You're not writing a novel; just write your thoughts and anything else you think is worth noting. Be sure to journal your thoughts when you actually stop to listen to them. Try not to be making breakfast, letting the dog out, and waking the kids up all at the same time while trying to observe/journal your thoughts.

When you feel comfortable in your ability to do this, start thought journaling at various points during the day. Maybe you write in your journal for a moment before you head out to work in the morning, again at lunchtime, and before you go to bed. As you practice, you will notice that you are becoming more and more comfortable with monitoring your thoughts and transferring them to paper.

When you feel comfortable in your abilities, start thought journaling at specific times. Journal your thoughts when you are in the midst of a stressful situation, when you feel distressed, and when you have just experienced a triumph. Most importantly, journal your thoughts while you are working on your goals and objectives. After completing an objective, stop and listen to your thoughts. "I did great!" or "I can do this" might be your thoughts. Don't forget to journal thoughts after failures too: "This will never work" or "I am not good enough to do this" could be examples. Journaling your negative thoughts will probably tell you a little more about your psyche than positive thoughts.

Right now I suggest that you take a break from reading and spend at least a couple days journaling your thoughts. Why should you do this? When you first start journaling you will likely see a barrage of random thoughts that seem to have no rhyme or reason. Over the course of time, you will probably begin to notice a pattern. There will be a couple of thoughts that keep recurring time and time again. These thoughts are oftentimes very strongly tied to our core beliefs and hold great power over the way we see ourselves, others, and the world around us. Don't worry if these thoughts are negative because we all have them (recovering pessimist, remember?). It is a very good thing if you can identify a core negative thought or thoughts because we are going to make a plan for change!

OK, I am assuming now that you have been journaling your thoughts for at least a couple of days, and it's time to do what human beings are best at: judging stuff. You are going to judge the crap out of the thoughts you have been journaling (especially the core thoughts) and determine whether they are helpful or harmful, rational or irrational.

Be wary of these irrational and harmful thoughts. To help you identify which thoughts are irrational and harmful, here are the typical categories these thoughts fall into. It is so important to remember that it is *normal* for you have these thoughts; I have them too. Do not feel bad or defeated in any way for thinking like this because it is natural. Focus on the positives; identifying the problem is the first step to fixing it. What we are trying to accomplish is a new perspective and insight into the way we think, which will allow us to make changes. Pay specific attention to these categories and really question whether or not you engage in these types of thoughts.

- **Filtering**: filtering is when you experience something and filter out the good from the situation, focusing only on the negative. For example, let's say you went to the doctor for a physical. Your results showed that you are perfectly healthy, but it was noted that you are "slightly overweight." For a person engaging in filtering, the "slightly overweight" part is all he or she can think about even though the rest of the results were positive! Rational and realistic thinking would consider both the positive and negative aspects of a situation.

- **Overgeneralizing**: this is when one negative event is believed to be the start of a never-ending pattern. For example, let's say that instead of going out for dinner you decide to cook for your family. Everything is going great until you burn dinner to a crisp. At this point you may think to yourself, "I am a terrible cook and cannot do anything right for my family!" Even though this event happened just one time, overgeneralizing tends to make you feel as if it is an always-occurring phenomenon. Overgeneralization is also usually characterized by the use of absolutes. Absolutes are words such as "always," "never," "every time," and "nobody." Absolutes are generally not true because there are usually exceptions. Pay attention to your thoughts and the language of your thoughts. If you think in terms of absolutes, then chances are that you are engaging in overgeneralization. Rational and realistic thinking would recognize that just because there was a disappointing outcome this time does not mean that the outcome will always be disappointing.

- **All or nothing thinking**: this type of thinking sees the world in extremes. There is no middle ground with this type of thinking. You are either smart or stupid, skinny or fat, successful or a failure. One example would be if you started a new medication and began to feel better than you had been but not as well as you felt before you got sick. Therefore, you tell yourself that the medicine has failed. Rational and realistic thinking can see the world from the middle and stay away from extremes.

- **Catastrophizing**: this is when you view a current situation as being a predictor for future disaster. If you have a hard time imagining what catastrophizing is, just think back to being in seventh grade. Or maybe you have kids or someone you know has kids that age.

When you are in that age range, everything negative that happens is "the end of the world." If your boyfriend or girlfriend breaks up with you, *"I'll never love again!"* If you get grounded for two days, *"I am always in trouble!"* These are extreme examples, but we also engage in this type of thinking as adults. Let's say that you have back pain that brings about discomfort, but it is bearable. You may think, "In ten years, I will not be able to walk!" Rational and realistic thinking involves objectively seeing situations for their future likelihood, not the worst case scenario.

- **Labeling**: labeling is when you call yourself insulting names or speak in a demeaning way to yourself. Oftentimes you would never talk to another person this way, but for some reason it seems OK to talk to yourself using these words. "Stupid," "idiot," "useless," and "worthless" are just a few. If you are anything like me, you will occasionally throw some four-letter words at yourself just for added effect. Rational and realistic thinking says that using insulting labels is not fair and can be hurtful, even to ourselves.

- **Mind-reading**: this is a big one, especially for those of us who tend to be a little on the neurotic side. Engaging in mind-reading means that you think you know what others are thinking about you, and it is always negative. Have you ever been giving a speech or a presentation and heard someone in the room laughing? For those of us who are a little neurotic (raising my hand), it is almost impossible to just brush it off. You immediately start thinking, "They're laughing at me. What did I say? What did I do? Do I have a booger?" You are reacting to what your own imagination tells you about what others are thinking and then creating negative thought patterns. Rational and healthy thinking says that guessing what others think about you is likely to be inaccurate, so why bother? Also, who gives a rip if they are laughing at you?

- **Shouldys and musturbation**: "shoulds" and "musts" are especially difficult to overcome, mostly because our "shoulds" and "musts" are ingrained from our childhoods. "Shoulds" and "musts" refer to our beliefs about the world, others, and ourselves. These types of thoughts include "Wives *should* cook dinner every night," "I *must* own a house because renting is unacceptable," "My doctor *should* spend at least half an hour with me when I visit." Sometimes shoulds and musts represent healthy ideals that have been passed down from our family. The problem is that even positive shoulds and musts represent rigid thinking and do not give us much room for change and adaptability. Rational and realistic thinking understands that there are limitations to the world and yourself. The world is not always fair, and we may have to let go of some of our shoulds and musts.

When covering the concept of total behavior earlier, we learned that our thinking, actions, feelings, and physiology are all connected. All of these components make up total behavior, but we have the most control over our actions and our thoughts. It's time to rewire your thought processes.

Do you remember our car analogy for total behavior earlier? Thoughts and actions make up the front wheels (connected by an axle) and feelings/physiology make up the rear wheels (also connected by an axle). When you turn the steering wheel of a car, you turn the front wheels. Wherever those wheels go, the back wheels have no choice but to follow. This chapter is how you get your hands on the steering wheel and take control. I am not just asking you to be aware of your thoughts, but also to make specific judgments about them. When a thought enters your mind, stop what you are doing and ask yourself, "Is this thought helping to move me toward my goal or away from it?" If your thought is moving you away from your goal, stop and redirect your thoughts. Another question you should ask yourself is, "Am I worrying or thinking about things that are within my control?" Remember, you are responsible for your total behavior and no one else's. If you are worrying about something you can control, take action. If not, redirect your thoughts. When you are evaluating and journaling your thoughts, write down the irrational or unhealthy thought. Next to the thought, write down which category of cognitive distortions your thoughts fall into. Think about a possible alternative thought that is more rational and write it down. If you get stuck, ask yourself these questions about your thought process.

- Would most people I know agree with this thought? If not, what would they think?
- What would I say to a friend if he or she were in a similar situation?
- What will happen if I continue to think this way?

---

## Thrive Thought:

We (human beings) spend so much time on autopilot that we just do what comes naturally, including our thought processes. You have to combat the negative and complacent thinking that has been such a huge factor in keeping you from reaching your goals. Here is a breakdown of your plan.

1. Learn to observe your thoughts by taking the time to listen to them.
2. Identify core thoughts through thought journaling (or any thoughts if you don't reach the core ones), especially those surrounding your goals for change.
3. Identify the cognitive distortion (don't you feel so smart saying cognitive distortion):

---

labeling, over generalizing, filtering, catastrophizing, musturbating, etcetera.

4. Write down the evidence that supports your
core thought and the evidence that does
not support it. *Be honest.*

5. Grab the steering wheel: replace your irrational thought with a more rational one that
is grounded in evidence and truth.

6. *Thrive!*

# CHAPTER 16

# If You're Happy Would You Know It?

As we discussed previously, feelings are very powerful. They can hit us like a tidal wave and quickly drown us if we are not proactive. There are thousands of feelings available within the human experience, and just the act of labeling them is probably an exercise in futility. Trying to understand these feelings can prove even more difficult. So how then do we know what feelings we are experiencing? Typically we divide feelings into three different categories: good, bad, and neutral. Dividing our feelings into these three fairly broad categories makes understanding and labeling our feelings a bit more doable; and we like doable.

To understand and ultimately gain more control over our feelings, it is important to note that feelings are relegated to two distinct levels. The first level is the automatic feeling. These are the feelings that we cannot control. Something in our environment changes or someone affects our life and we react. Let's say that you are driving on a busy highway, minding your own business. It is rush hour, and traffic is terrible. You had a very busy day at work, and that headache just won't go away. You are fumbling with the radio when traffic begins to open up and you begin moving. You are thinking about what to cook for dinner and games you are going to play with your kids when...*look out*! A car swerves into your lane and runs you off the road. What feelings are you experiencing? Anxiety, panic, fear, and shock hit you all at once. You are able to pull safely off the road, and the car that ran you off comes to a stop fifty yards away at a stop light.

Your feelings of anxiety, panic, fear, and shock? They are automatic feelings. You did not have to think about having these feelings, and you did not consciously choose to feel them. They are simply your response to a situation. The feelings that come after the automatic ones are called secondary feelings. Let's go back to our scenario. You get out of your car and think, "That jerk! S/he almost killed me!" Now feelings of anger and rage come in quickly. Not even thinking about it, you sprint up to the car, ready to knock someone's block off. You get to the car...and there is a woman in the back seat in labor—and she needs to be at a hospital *now*. The driver looks scared and way too young to be driving. He apologizes profusely and begs for help. Now what are your feelings/emotions?

It is important to remember that feelings serve a purpose. They are not just pesky little nuances of the human existence whose only purpose is to get us in trouble. Our minds and bodies produce feelings for very good reasons. Fear serves to keep us safe from danger, protect us, and keep us vigilant. Anxiety tells us that something is wrong and serves as a warning to the rest of our body. Anger prepares us to attack and usually brings with it a surge of adrenaline to provide strength.

Feelings are not something to be done away with entirely; they just need to be channeled. Our automatic feelings are completely outside of our control, but the secondary emotions are usually a result of our thoughts or actions. In the above scenario, the panic, fear, etcetera are natural responses to what has occurred. The rage that followed was a result of thoughts about the situation, and maybe that rage felt justified at the time. However, further inspection of the situation revealed something else entirely. You should never feel bad or like a failure because of automatic feelings. They are truly outside of your control and a function of a healthy human being.

It is worth noting that feelings are something a person experiences; they do not constitute the whole person. You are not your feelings, and they most certainly do not control you. The most mature and appropriate secondary feeling is one that falls into the neutral category. This does not just happen though. As with our thoughts, we have become desensitized and numb to our feelings. As a result, we are often on autopilot and subject to the whims of our secondary feelings. We become so used to living our lives this way that we become disassociated from our feelings and have difficulty even labeling them.

So what is the solution? Be *mindful* of your feelings. When you are in a stressful situation, notice and attempt to accurately label what your feelings are in the situation. Do not judge them or feel bad about having them; you do not control them. Pay very close attention to the internal thoughts and external actions that follow those automatic feelings. These will go a long way in determining your secondary feelings.

**Thrive Thought:**

You do not have direct control over your feelings, but you can gain control indirectly through your thoughts and actions. Experiencing an emotion usually leads to irrational thinking, and that's not what we want. Irrational thoughts lead to actions not based on fact and then feelings based on those actions, so on and so forth. So what do we do? Cut it off at the source. Here is your action plan for handling feelings.

1. Recognize and label your feelings.
2. Be aware of whether this is a primary or secondary emotion. Primary emotions are

automatic; secondary emotions happen after thoughts/actions follow primary emotions.

3. Don't fight your primary emotions—feel them. Remember that your emotions also serve a positive function.

4. Do *not* make any big decisions while experiencing a strong emotion (this goes for positive emotions too).

5. Be mindful of your thoughts and watch your actions—do something to take control of the situation away from your emotions.

# CHAPTER 17

# Fake It 'Til You Make It

I am hoping that by now when I say total behavior, you know exactly what I'm talking about. This is one of the key points of *The Thrive Life*: *total behavior includes actions, thoughts, feelings, and physiology. All are connected, and a change in one area leads to a change in all.* We only have direct control over our thoughts and actions, with actions being the easiest to change.

We have already covered how to observe, judge, challenge, and change your thoughts. Working on your thoughts is a great way to take control over your total behavior and point your car in the right direction, but there is an easier way. Have you ever tried to drive a car without power steering? Power steering is one of those wonderful technological advances that you can never truly appreciate until you experience life without it. Allow me to paint the picture if you have never driven without power steering. You are driving along and everything is cool; as long as you are driving straight. You come to a red light and it's time to turn. You have to lift your entire body into the air and use every bit of torque you can muster just to get into the turn lane. You basically have to be the Incredible Hulk to get around corners. Changing your total behavior through your thoughts is driving your total behavior car without power steering—you can control it and make turns, but boy it's hard. Don't get me wrong; it's certainly doable with practice and grit, but it can be difficult. There is an easier way, friend: your actions. Do you want that car to turn nice and easy with little resistance? Change your actions.

How do you change your actions? Pretend you have the life you want, also known as fake it 'til you make it. It's OK; I know you probably haven't pretended in a long time, but it's time to reactivate your imagination. I realize that this does not sound like professional advice, but this is actually an incredibly effective therapeutic tool. In therapy circles we call it "acting as if," mostly because "fake it 'til you make it" doesn't really sound all that academic...and you know how important it is for therapists to feel smart (laughing a little). So what is this "acting as if"?

Imagine how your life would be different and how you would behave after achieving your goals, and then act as if this has happened. Let's use our example goal again: "be healthier" (with one effect being improved self-confidence). Ask yourself, "What does a self-confident person look like? How does a self-confident person walk? How does he or she talk? What specific behaviors does he or she use? How do these people handle conflict?" Think about it—then pretend. Self-confident people smile, look other people in the eyes, walk tall with their shoulders back; they engage others in conversation and approach conflict calmly. These questions and answers can be applied to any goals, allowing you to "act as if" you have achieved any personal goal.

What if your goal is to be a better spouse? We have a prime example of "acting as if" in The Love Dare. The Love Dare was made popular by the movie *Fireproof.* In the movie, a man's marriage is in the dumps, and he cannot seem to repair it despite his best efforts. He is trying and trying to change the way his wife sees him, but he is not only failing, he is making things worse. His father then tells him about The Love Dare, which is something the father used when he was younger to save his marriage. The Love Dare is a month-long commitment in which each day brings a new "dare." One dare is "Say nothing negative to your spouse," another is "Buy your spouse something that says 'I love you,'" and another is "Think of something your spouse needs and lift that burden from him or her." This goes on for a month, and the results are incredibly positive. The Love Dare asks the question (without actually asking), "How would you act if your marriage was perfect?" The dares that follow lead you to "acting as if" your marriage *is* perfect. This stuff works, people! I am not advertising The Love Dare, but the principles behind it are solid. The point is that you cannot ever change other people, but you are always in control of yourself.

# Fake It 'Til You Make It

You may feel a little disingenuous by "acting as if"—like you are lying. At first you will likely feel this way and may even feel silly pretending. Don't worry because the feeling silly phase will pass. Pretty soon you will see results and actually feel the way you have been pretending to feel, and at that point it's not pretending anymore. Remember to pretend with positive behaviors and character traits, but please don't pretend to have skills or talents you do not yet have. We all laugh at the fast-food coffee Styrofoam cups that say, "Warning, this hot drink is hot." Those disclaimers are there for a reason though. This is my version of the "Warning, the hot coffee is hot so please do not dump it on your face" disclaimer. If one of your goals is to achieve a master's degree in engineering, don't act as if you have a degree and apply for jobs with that on your resume. Not good. Don't sprint onto an airfield and hop into the cockpit of a helicopter to act as if you know how to fly. Not good. Do not act as if you can complete an ironman triathlon if you have never trained a day in your life. Also not good. I think you get the point here: use good judgment.

## Thrive Work

Pull out your goals again…it's time for work! Take a good look at them and imagine how you would behave if each of those goals was achieved. Write down some behaviors a person who has achieved those goals would engage in, and don't be afraid to get specific. Here are my examples.

1. Be a better husband and father. How would I act if I was a better husband and father?
   - I would treat my wife with love and respect no matter how angry or upset I am, including:
     - Telling her I love her every day.
     - Refusing to say anything negative to her.
   - I would spend more time with my kids, including:
     - Playing with them when they ask me to more often than not playing with them.
     - Engaging myself in activities *they* enjoy, not just things for me.
   - I would have more patience with my wife and children, including:
     - Allowing them to make mistakes without criticizing.
     - Purposefully engaging with my wife in assertive communication instead of authoritarian or passive.
2. Achieve a graduate degree. How would I act if I achieved a graduate degree?
   - I would have more confidence in my intellect, including:
     - Looking people in the eye when speaking with them.
     - Confidently sharing my opinions.
   - I would be more responsible with my finances, including:
     - Balancing my checkbook monthly to track expenses.
     - Creating a budget to ensure I live within my means.

- I would be happier with my work, including:
  - ➢ Purposefully being friendly with my coworkers.
  - ➢ Doing the best work I can and understanding that my work is important.
3. Be healthier. How would I act if I was healthier?
  - I would make better decisions with food and exercise, including:
    - ➢ Making small changes to improve what I eat and drink.
    - ➢ Looking for opportunities to exercise more than before (taking stairs instead of elevator, parking farther from the office, etcetera).
  - I would have more self-confidence in my appearance, including:
    - ➢ Walking tall with my shoulders back.
    - ➢ Refusing to focus on aspects I don't like about my appearance and placing importance on the aspects I do like.
  - I would have more energy, including:
    - ➢ Playing with my children more often.
    - ➢ Making time for an exercise regimen.

Remember, actions are the easiest part of total behavior to manipulate. By taking control of your actions by acting as if, you are likely to find that your thoughts will follow. Before long, you will notice your feelings and physiology following suit. It will feel strange at first, almost as if you are pretending to be someone else. That is expected, and you will get used to it over time.

**Thrive Thought:**

This is just like all of the other exercises presented so far...this will not come easy and it takes practice. I have thrown a lot of exercises at you so far; which ones should you try first? Start with your actions—acting as if. Once you have done this, move on to observing, journaling, and challenging your thoughts. Actions and thoughts are the only two components of total behavior we can control, with actions being the easiest. Focus on actions first.

# CHAPTER 18

# Keep An Eye On Your GPS

Your total behavior car is rolling now! You have learned to take control of your actions and thoughts and, by doing so, have also taken control of your feelings and physiology. That is fantastic! But how do you know if you're driving your car in the right direction? In order to know if you are moving toward or away from your objectives and goals, you have to develop some way to track your progress.

Imagine that you are taking a class in college. You walk in the first day extremely nervous about the workload because this is a core course. The professor steps up and proclaims that there is no homework. *Woo-hoo!* Looking around you can see a little smile creep up on everyone's face. That sounds awesome, right? Well, guess what? The professor then announces that there are not any papers either. *Yes!* You will only be graded on one exam: the final exam, which is to be taken the last day of class. When you are in class the professor lectures for three hours and then sends you on your merry way. The professor does not provide you with an e-mail address or phone number, and he or she does not have office hours. You show up the last day of class and it is time for the final exam. You have not done any homework, written any papers, taken any other tests, or corresponded with the professor in any way. Maybe you pass the final and succeed, but that's not likely. You have had absolutely no way to track your learning throughout the semester. You do not have a clue what to expect on the final exam, and you do your best guessing when you get there.

Why would you be so lost on this exam? The purpose of homework and various assignments throughout a class is to measure your learning and challenge you to go deeper into the subject matter. Without these measuring sticks, you have no idea where you stand when it is test time! How much greater would your chances be of passing the class if you had ways to measure your progress throughout the semester? In a similar way, it is very important that we constantly measure our progress (or lack thereof) when striving to achieve goals and objectives. Otherwise, how will we know how we are doing? If your car took a wrong turn somewhere on the path to achieving your goals, you would have to be paying attention to know to turn around!

You need a way to measure your progress, and I've got some ideas. Effective measuring of our progress, including details of what works and what does not work, is crucial. One of the best ways to measure your progress is to use scales.

# Keep An Eye On Your GPS

Scaling is a great way to add a measurable component to something not easily measured (progress toward goals). What does that mean? The goals we want to achieve are sometimes written in abstract terms. Our objectives are put into concrete terms that are easily measurable, but scaling is a great way to measure overall life progress as opposed to specific objective and goal progress.

How do you scale something? The process is very simple. The first thing you need to do is define what you are measuring. For me, scaling was a great way to measure how I felt about my overall health. The second step is to set up your scaling parameters. I like to use a scale of one through five, but you can stretch yours out to one hundred if you feel like being crazy. The next step is to decide what each number represents. Obviously, on a scale of one through five, three is neutral (this is why one through five may be preferable). A three would represent no real progress, but also no regression. I set up my numbers this way.

- 1 = Try again tomorrow
- 2 = Not great
- 3 = Neutral
- 4 = Good day
- 5 = *Oh yeah!*

You can obviously set up your numbers to represent any phrase or wording you like, but these worked great for me. It is important that you commit to at least *daily* tracking of your progress. I say at least daily because you could certainly scale more, such as every meal, every hour, morning/noon/night, etcetera. The simplest way to do this is to write the number on a calendar or just put the number in your calendar on your phone. After tracking your progress for some time, at least a month, take notice of trends in your data; there will be trends. Do you notice that there are particular days that are always one number or another? This is not unusual because we tend to have behavior patterns that are on autopilot, behaviors we have become comfortable with. You may notice that some entire weeks are better than others, and that is OK as well. There will certainly be ebbs and flows to your progress. When you find that you have a particular day of the week that is consistently better or worse than the other days, ask yourself, "What is different about those days? What happens to make me more/less successful?" These are important questions because you could potentially replicate what it is that makes you successful on those days or possibly eliminate what causes you to fall short.

For example, you may find that Tuesdays are always "try again tomorrow" days. Think about those days and what is different. Perhaps on Tuesdays you have staff meetings that last all day, and by the time you can eat you usually binge on snack foods from the vending machine because you are starving. Maybe after work on Tuesdays your child has soccer practice and you have to rush over right after work. The stress of your Tuesday staff meetings sticks with you, not to mention the fact that you don't even have time to make it home to change before heading to soccer. The result is that you are completely stressed and worn out at the end of soccer practice, so the family eats out...and you want some comfort food! Dairy Queen, here we come! You can effectively plan and strategize if you spot trends and know what to expect. Maybe you pack a few healthy snacks to eat throughout the day during your staff meetings. Perhaps you adjust for your stress, taking five minutes before leaving work to engage in some stress relieving breathing exercises.

Noticing a trend (even a bad trend) is a *good* thing; this means you can get in there and fix whatever the issue is. In the same way, if you notice that Thursdays are always "Oh yeah" days, what is going on with Thursdays? Well, as you look into it you may notice that you pack your lunch on Wednesday nights, giving you some free time Thursday mornings. Perhaps on Thursdays you jog during your lunch break, or maybe you are able to catch up with your work on Thursdays, relieving some stress. Whatever it is, whatever works, *do it*! Find a way to replicate the behaviors, thoughts, etcetera that lead to your success and repeat!

## Thrive Work:

OK, now it is time to talk about tracking your progress with your specific objectives. Still have your goals and objectives that you wrote down? Good. Go make some copies and put spaces below each objective. I suggest having one goal per page to allow for plenty of space. You will have (at most) three sheets of paper to work with. As you work toward the completion of your objectives, just jot down what days you did what you set out to do. For anything that does not apply at the time, just put N/A below it so you remember that the particular objective couldn't be completed. This is where the continuous work comes in. You will need to print out a copy of your goals and objectives weekly to measure your progress. Here is an example of what yours may look like.

Week of Oct. 15–22
1. Be a better husband and father
   · Spend two hours a night playing with my children at least four nights a week for the next six months
     * Oct. 25 two hours
     * Oct. 26 two hours
     * Oct. 28 one hour
     * Oct. 29 two hours
   · Go on a date night with my wife (just the two of us) three nights a month for the next six months
     * None this week
   · Go on one family vacation over the next six months that lasts at least three days
     * Began discussions with spouse about possible dates and locations

· Attend at least 80 percent (four out of five) of my children's sporting events/school functions over the next six months

- Attended only function this week: baseball game on Oct. 27

· Prepare dinners at home at least four nights a week for the next six months

- Home dinners on Oct. 25, Oct. 26, Oct. 28, and Oct. 29

2. Achieve a graduate degree

· Register for and take the GRE (Graduate Record Examination) within the next three months

- Registered for GRE

· Of the classes I register for, attend at least 90 percent of the class meetings

- N/A

· Spend at least one hour a night, four nights a week, studying or completing assignments

- N/A

· Complete all assignments at least three days before they are due

- N/A

· Apply for at least three scholarships.

- N/A

3. Be healthier

· Calculate my basal metabolic rate to determine how many calories I should be taking in daily by the end of this week

- Researched how to calculate basal metabolic rate—not done yet.

· Research at-home exercise programs (P90x, INSANITY, etcetera), make a decision, and purchase one by the end of next week

- Began research on exercise programs—none purchased

· Begin walking five days a week for half an hour, either before or after work

- Oct. 25 half an hour
- Oct. 26 half an hour
- Oct. 27 half an hour

· Educate myself by reading at least two books about nutrition and physical health within the next six months

- Not started yet

· Schedule a physical within the next month

- Not done yet

Yes, this can be tedious. Yes, this is very difficult. And yes, it is most certainly worth it. Fill out your sheets every week and keep them, whether you save them in a binder or keep an electronic copy on your computer. When you complete an objective, line it out and feel free to celebrate! This should be treated as a huge accomplishment; you are making wonderful progress! If tracking your objectives in this way is too much work, and for some it is, feel free to use the scaling system detailed previously as a substitute. If you made some progress on your goal but did not make as much progress as you wanted to, give your day a 4 (good day). If you made no progress but also did not regress, give your day a 3 (neutral), and so on. You can do this or feel free to create your own way of measuring progress. *What tool you use to measure your progress is far less important than you being consistent with the tool you select.*

Think of it in terms of measuring your weight on an electronic scale. You have one at your house, and it says you are a certain weight. Later that day you are at a friend's house and weigh yourself on his or her electronic scale. You gained ten pounds! What the what? Probably not—your apparent weight change is due to differences in the devices used to measure weight. Imagine if you were measuring your weight changes over a six-month period and you were switching between different scales. That would be insanely frustrating! Likewise, do not flip between different ways of measuring your progress because the inconsistency will drive you mad and skew your results. As you settle in on a way of tracking your progress, it will get easier as you continue.

**Thrive Thought:**

I've said it before, and I'll say it again: *this is a lot of information*. Please take the time you need to truly digest this and understand how to apply it to your own life. Scaling your general goal direction is a great way to measure your progress when tracking objectives is just too hard. Don't beat yourself up if that is the case; just do what works.

# CHAPTER 19

# I'm Good Enough,
# I'm Smart Enough...

Mantras are statements or personal sayings that are usually short and repeated over and over. The word "mantra" was first developed to represent Hindu sayings spoken repeatedly during meditation. Don't freak out—you do not have to meditate or ascribe to any particular religion to use or benefit from a mantra. For me, mantras were akin to mindfulness just a few short years ago (back on the Tibetan mountain with the goats). Once I let go of my own biases surrounding the word, I realized that there are solid reasons for having a mantra.

Developing a mantra may seem silly to you at first, and it definitely did for me. A word or phrase you repeat over and over? All I could think about when I was first working on my mantra was Al Franken on *Saturday Night Live*. He played a character named Stuart Smalley who would stare at the camera and say, "I'm good enough, I'm smart enough, and, dog-gonnit, people like me." Yes, I felt just like Stuart Smalley when thinking of a mantra. He would get that cheesy look on his face and peer into the mirror—man it was funny. That's not what you have to do!

Your mantra is your own, and it can be whatever you want it to be. Make it something meaningful, something you will remember to say daily that will help you remain focused. Some examples are "It is what it is," "I create my happiness," "I am in control," "If it is to be, it is up to me," "Yes indeed, I succeed," "Luck is the intersection of hard work and opportunity," and "Everything happens for a reason." Your mantra does not have to rhyme, and it really does not have to be some sort of deep, philosophical saying. I have had several mantras over the course of the last six years. One of mine was "GROW!" It was in all caps with an exclamation point, just like that. I wrote it down and put it in various places that I would be sure to notice throughout the day. It reminded me to stretch myself and find some way to grow every single day. Another of my mantras came from a quote I read: "I saw injustice in the world and said, 'Somebody should do something about that.' Then I realized that I am somebody." The mantra I developed from this quote was "I am somebody." It sounds as if this mantra would help me engage in self-affirmation, but it was really a reminder for my spirit. This mantra helped remind me daily that there are others in the world, and I should be constantly aware of opportunities to affect change. My latest mantra came from my passion for sports, and I developed it to help me with my health and fitness goals. "Get the W." It is short, and it is motivating for me. "Get the W." I wrote this down and put it everywhere I would see it; I even made it the background for my phone. I used this as a reminder of how I was measuring my progress toward my goals. If I got a four or a five on my daily scaling, that was a win, a "W." If I got a three or less on my scale, that would go down as a loss, an "L." My thinking was that if I had two wins for every loss, I would certainly succeed in my fitness goals.

There are no rules for developing your mantra; just find something that works for you. Make it something you can write down, repeat to yourself over and over, and use for motivation. Once you write it down, put it in places that you will see it regularly. Maybe you could put it on the mirror in your bathroom, the dash of your car, or on your screensaver. There is nothing mystical or magical about developing a mantra; it just helps to keep you focused and motivated. It also has a strong psychological foundation. What do you suppose will happen if you repeat a word or phrase to yourself daily? That's right: you might actually begin to believe in it. Friend, by developing a mantra you have just grabbed the steering wheel of your car by changing your thoughts. See? This all makes sense, I promise.

**Thrive Thought:**
Of all the exercises and suggestions thus far, this one is the simplest. Find a word or phrase that is particularly motivating to you—repeat it! You will eventually believe in your mantra, and your actions, feelings, and physiology will follow suit. You can do this!

# CHAPTER 20

# Visualize

Visualization is a powerful therapy technique that is very helpful when trying to achieve goals, and you have more experience in this than you think. We often see pictures or images in our mind that appear or just seem to pop up from time to time. Sometimes we see images from our past, and sometimes our minds and imaginations wander to what the future could hold. Have you ever planned a vacation? It is amazing what visualizations can occur just from making future plans. Planning for a vacation is a perfect example of this. You can close your eyes and imagine the crashing ocean waves on a cruise ship, the smell of sunscreen on the deck of the boat, and the taste of a perfectly made cocktail.

Even something as simple as getting ready for work or school in the morning can include visualization. As you are getting dressed, you may imagine sitting at your desk, preparing for the day. You may recognize certain smells, sounds, or sights in your visualization. We don't call this "visualization" in everyday life; we instead call it daydreaming. We call it this mostly because we tend to see it as unproductive. What if we put the full power of our imagination to work, using it to propel us toward prosperity and success? Could it work? I know what you are thinking: "How is daydreaming going to help me achieve my goals?" Just thinking about conquering a stressful situation can make it less stressful; mentally preparing for a difficult conversation can help things flow more smoothly.

I am talking about taking another step though. In visualization you *have* to engage as many of your five senses as possible. Warning: this will be weird at first (a lot of these exercises are). Try your best to envision sights, sounds, smells, tastes, and touch. Why? The more senses you engage the more neural connections are made and the more real the scenario becomes. Hint: this is another exercise that allows you to take control of your thoughts.

Visualization is an exercise that is great to do in the mornings before you have really started your day. Pull out your goals and take a good look at them. Read them out loud, one at a time. As you read one, close your eyes and begin to imagine your life after you have completed your goal. Visualize as much detail as possible, and remember to engage all five senses. You should also try to include your emotions in the moment (how you feel), and do not be afraid to make your visualization "perfect." Life will not be perfect just because you achieve your goals, but it is OK for your visualization to be insanely positive. That's the idea! Every day you use visualizations, you do not have to use the same ones. In fact, I would encourage you to visualize several different scenarios of your life after you have achieved your goals. I will use my goals as examples, and my visualizations are ridiculous (they're supposed to be).

1. Be a better father and husband

   I close my eyes and imagine myself at home, cooking dinner. It is spaghetti night, and I just pulled the garlic bread out of the oven. The warm air from the oven envelopes my face as my nose is inundated with the wonderful smell of melted butter, garlic salt, and garlic powder cooked together on a fresh piece of Italian-style bread. My wife comes home and squeezes my hand gently, leaving her fingers intertwined with mine. She asks how my day was and leans in to give me a kiss. We kiss and embrace. Behind her I hear the sound of little feet rushing toward me and hear, "Daddy!" It's my kids, and the smiles on their faces from seeing their dad is the most wonderful thing I have seen all day long. I feel joyous and almost overwhelmed by the wonderful love shown to me by my family. "Daddy, let's go play!" my kids shout excitedly. My wife agrees to take over dinner so I can play and off we go.

2. Achieve a graduate degree

I close my eyes and imagine myself walking into a job interview. It is a cool, crisp day outside, and it feels good to step indoors. Just before I get in the doors, I do a quick double-check to make sure my breath is fresh. All clear and still minty fresh. As I come through the doors, I catch the eye of a couple of other people waiting for their turn to interview. I look better, and I know it. I quickly check my tie again. Yes, still perfect. The other people look a little nervous sitting and waiting, especially more so since I walked in. I have the confidence and the look of someone with an advanced degree. Two people, a man and a woman, call me back for my interview, and I smile confidently as I walk back. I introduce myself with a confident voice and give a firm handshake, maintaining consistent eye contact. I sit down and open my briefcase to pull out my résumé. I can feel the crisp paper on my fingers as I pull the résumé out for my interviewers to see. As they read through my credentials, I see one of them mouth the word, "Wow." The interview begins, and I answer all the questions confidently and competently. I can tell that the interviewers are impressed, and I feel a great deal of pride in having absolutely nailed the interview. As I walk out of the interview, I am told, "Expect a call soon." I smile and say, "Thank you, I look forward to your call." I stroll out of the building twirling my keys with a smile on my face that cannot be wiped off.

3. Be healthier

I close my eyes and imagine myself at the beach. I came out with my wife and family, but the beach is crowded today. It is an absolutely perfect day. It is hot enough to spend the day at the beach but not so hot that it is uncomfortable. If there was some kind of outdoor thermostat, this is the temperature everyone would agree on. As I stroll toward the beach, I kick my flip-flops off and feel the sand beneath my feet. Some of the sand goes between my toes, and the cool sand makes my feet feel more comfortable than any shoes ever have. The smell of sunscreen is in the air, and I can still feel some stuck to my arm. My family and I get settled in the perfect spot, set up our umbrella, and pull out our lunch. I decide to take my shirt off to get ready to go swimming. As I take my shirt off, the people passing by seem to stop and notice. Even my family seems surprised about how good I look. My wife stands up and comes close, letting everyone else know that I am hers. She beams with pride as she holds me close. My brother and I start throwing the football on the beach, and pretty soon some other guys join in. I notice that the other guys seem to be getting winded already, but I am just hitting my stride. It only takes ten minutes before everyone seems to recognize that I am the superior athlete. I can jump higher, run faster, and run farther than any of the others. At one point a Hail Mary is thrown up for the win. I size up the other players and the trajectory of the ball, sprinting from out of nowhere and diving to make the most spectacular catch of the day. I land face-first in the sand and get a mouthful. The sand tastes gritty, and my elbows are stinging from where I landed, but I hold onto the ball and win the game. Suddenly the taste of sand isn't so bad and seems to signify my triumph. I feel great pride in myself as all the hard work I put in has paid off. I race over to the shower to wash the sand free and head back to the tent with my family to start on lunch.

OK, so you might have noticed that there was just a pinch of vanity present in those stories (no, that's really not what I think of myself), and there should be. Live vicariously through your visualizations and do not be afraid to come across as a little selfish. The idea behind the visualization is that your goal has been accomplished and everything is perfect, not necessarily realistic. Visualize your success daily and try to include as much detail as possible.

**Thrive Thought:**

Visualization is another exercise that is easy to do; all the work takes place in your own imagination! It's also kind of fun to pretend and imagine your life after you have accomplished your goals. You will find as you engage your senses that the scenarios become very real. As you work toward your objectives and goals, your visualizations can become your happy places. They can be places for you to go when things get difficult and you don't feel like pressing forward. Engage your senses and imagine your life with your goals completed; this is great motivation!

# CHAPTER 21

# Simmer Down Now!

Setting goals, making big changes, and striving to become a better person can be stressful. Don't kid yourself; this is going to be difficult (but oh so worth it). Your life was most likely stressful before you made the decision to maximize your potential, and now you have added all these goals, objectives, and exercises into the mix. The best way to handle stress is to realize that stress is a natural part of life and necessary. Stress is your body's way of letting you know that something is about to happen. Stress happens, and it should happen. The problem is when our physiological response (stress) is compounded and worsened by our own thoughts (I will never overcome this), feelings (despair), and actions (dominating a bag of Doritos). Take control of your total behavior, reduce the stress, and overcome.

Coming to this realization will not eliminate stress in your life, but it will reverse the downward trend. You will gain power over your stress instead of your stress having power over you. Having stress in your life is nothing to be ashamed of and something we all experience. Stress and anxiety are normal psychological and physiological responses to perceived threats. Our bodies are all wired with an internal alarm system, usually referred to as our "fight-or-flight" response. When our brain perceives (there's that perception again) a threat, the switch is flipped for the alarm, and hormones go rushing through our body to help us manage the threat. For a lot of people, when the threat leaves, our body returns to a normal state. Unfortunately, the stress and anxiety brought about by our on-the-go, microwaved lifestyle means that we are on alert far more often than we should be. There's the deadline for the work presentation, the kids have soccer practice, the in-laws are coming to visit tomorrow, the dog has a vet appointment today, and on and on and on. Now you have added these goals and objectives...what were you thinking?

Well, you may be shocked to find that working toward your goals actually provides you with some stress relief. What seems like it would only cause more stress (adding more stuff to your busy life) can actually *reduce* your stress! The exercises already outlined—i.e., mindfulness, thought journaling, visualization, acting "as if," staying positive, and developing mantras—are stress-relieving activities. Some great stress relievers may also be included in your objectives. Eating well, getting more sleep, exercising, spending time with your family, listening to music, and reading more are all wonderful stress-relieving activities. Forget the quantity of things in your life; focus on quality.

Do you recall the five basic human needs? They are love/belonging, power/accomplishment, freedom/independence, survival, and fun. Many times we want to look at basic human needs as existing on a pyramid or in some sort of hierarchy, where one is more important than another. If you were to put the five needs in a hierarchy, which would be the least important? Most people would say fun. Fun is one of those luxuries that we allow ourselves only if we finish our work and other duties. Instead of a hierarchy, it is more accurate to think of the human needs as the legs of a chair. All are equally important, and having one out of balance with the rest can be quite a problem. Fun is just as important as the others!

We often think, "There is no time for fun! I have too much work to do!" Trust me when I say that if you are fulfilling *all* of your needs (including fun), you will be much better at your job and more efficient. Did you get that? Take care of all your needs (including fun) and you will likely see the quality of your work rise! It is OK to schedule time for fun in your life, and your version of fun does not have to be anybody else's. For some, fun is reading a good book while others may enjoy playing with their kids or going skydiving. The point is to find out what you enjoy and start doing it! Even if your fun is as simple as setting a fantasy football lineup every week (like me); have fun!

# Simmer Down Now!

A large part of human stress comes from trying to control things that are outside of our control. You will feel a great deal of stress relief when you truly come to the realization of choice theory, which is "I am responsible for my behaviors. I can change myself, but I cannot change other people." Quit trying to change other people and your unchangeable environment, and instead focus all of your energy on what you can change: yourself. If you do this, you will notice a tremendous drop in your stress level. Don't be misled though; you will never be rid of stress completely.

What should we do with the remaining stress? Manage it. And your first step toward managing stress is to breathe. Breathing exercises are a great way to manage stress and help to calm you down. You probably have not taken the time to think about what breathing does for you because who stops to think about breathing? I certainly never did, mostly because breathing is not exactly something we do consciously. We just do it and have done it since the day we were born. Every inhale brings fresh oxygen into your lungs and bloodstream, and every exhale removes harmful waste. Different activity levels require different amounts of oxygen. When you are exercising, you need more oxygen and carbon dioxide. When you are relaxed, you need less of both. Now think about your breathing when you are stressed out. You tend to throw your breathing out of rhythm. Your rate of breathing becomes more rapid, and your breaths tend to be shallow. This change in the oxygen and carbon dioxide balance causes your body to react and can actually make your stress worse by bringing about physiological symptoms!

Taking control of your breathing through breathing exercises is a great tool for managing stress. Another wonderful thing about breathing exercises is that you may notice other benefits as well as anxiety and stress reduction. Regular breathing exercises can increase your energy, improve your mental focus, and improve your metabolism. Breathing exercises are simple and can be done in conjunction with some of the other exercises outlined already (see Chapter 14, "Be Mindful"). If you choose to engage in prayer or meditation, engaging in breathing exercises at the same time can be very fulfilling and aid in enriching your experience. You can engage in mindfulness exercises, take control of your thoughts, repeat your mantra, and use visualization all during your breathing exercises!

1. Basic breathing: sit or stand in a relaxed position. You are going to slowly inhale through your nose, counting to five in your head. Exhale through your mouth, counting to eight in your head as the air leaves your lungs. When you breathe, allow your abdomen to expand outward instead of raising your shoulders. You can do this set four or five times or stretch it out over several minutes.

2. Four-seven-eight breathing: sit or lie down in a relaxed position. Put one hand over your stomach and the other on your chest. Take a deep, slow breath from your abdomen and count in your head to four as you breathe in. Hold your breath and count in your head to seven. Breathe out completely as you count in your head to eight. Try to get all the air out of your lungs by the time you get to eight. You can repeat this as few or as many times as you like.

These two exercises can be very effective in targeting and reducing stress, but just mastering the basic breathing will bring about positive results. As you increase the amount of oxygen in your body, you will notice that you may be able to think more clearly (more oxygen to the brain) and have more energy (more oxygen to the muscles). Try to do at least the deep breathing exercise three times or more a day. As I said previously, it can be helpful to combine the deep breathing with other exercises such as visualization or prayer/meditation.

## Thrive Thought:

Just breathe! Stress is such a big factor in many of our lives that we basically just learn to live with it, not knowing that it can be managed. Consciously being aware of your breathing and choosing to perform breathing exercises is taking action, and actions are the most controllable component of total behavior. When you feel stressed ask yourself, "Can I control this situation?" If the answer is yes then take action. If the answer is no then ask yourself, "What can I control?" and focus on that. Remember that while you are adding a lot to your plate by striving for a thrive life, the exercises and activities should actually *reduce* your stress levels. Stick with it and make it happen!

# CHAPTER 22

# Know Your System

No one lives in a vacuum. Our every action affects others just as we are affected by the actions of other people around us. Every one of us lives and operates in systems. Systems emerge from our relationships and interactions with others and exist within our families, work environments, and social environments. You are making big changes here, and your changes won't affect only yourself. See beyond the linear line of thinking and expand your perspective to circular causality.

Linear thinking involves seeing ourselves and our actions in a vacuum; being unaffected by and having no direct effect on others. In this line of thinking, we see the world in terms of cause and effect, or A causes B. An example of this is a scenario in which a person may say, "My husband is controlling, and we constantly fight because I do not like this." Linear thinking sees this situation as "My husband is controlling and this causes me to react negatively." Circular causality sees the world through a pattern of interactions based on the reactions and perceived reactions of others. Describing a person and his or her behaviors involves a description that sees the person and his or her behavior as only one part of an interaction. A's behavior is a reaction to B's behavior, which is a reaction to A's behavior, and so on and so on. This becomes even more complicated when you add more participants to the system. From this perspective, patterns of interactions develop that promote predictability and stability in order to maintain balance in the system.

Let's take another look at our controlling husband through a circular causality perspective. Seeing his "controlling" behaviors through circular causality may reveal that his controlling behaviors are in response to the wife's perceived reckless behaviors. The wife then responds negatively to his control, and the husband responds with more controlling behaviors. Our behaviors are influenced by others and have a direct influence on how others respond to us. This is not to say that our decisions are controlled by others or that we can control other people. Understanding circular causality is the awareness that our behaviors and the behaviors of others have a much further-reaching effect than most of us know.

This is very important because any change you make in your life will invariably change your system. We as humans like stability and predictability; this is only natural. Our need for survival leads us to strive for homeostasis, or balance. We find balance within our family, social, and occupational systems through our interactions with others and their interactions with us. By making these changes in your life, you are seriously upsetting your system in a good way. Other people in your life will have no choice but to make changes because you have upset the system, and this can be positive or negative. There is no reason to fear because the system makes changes naturally over time as relationships grow and change. Also, most systems possess adaptability, which is the process of adjusting to changes without extremely negative consequences. The point of this chapter is not to scare you or discourage you from making changes but to make you aware of the possible outcomes of positive change in your life. Watch your system and the people in it and don't be surprised when they make changes too. Extremely positive change in your life (which you are making) will influence and promote positive change in the people within your system as well.

## Thrive Thought:

This chapter is more precautionary than any of the others. Your system will change—this is your warning. Don't be surprised when your changes influence others to change, whether directly or indirectly. Remember that this is not always a negative thing. Your positive change may be just what your family system needs to jumpstart a better lifestyle! Why should you make positive changes? The people you love are counting on you—more than you know.

# CHAPTER 23

## What If You Fail?

Ouch. An entire chapter dedicated to failure. This must be where I tell you that you are going to try valiantly, do your best, and then flame out less than halfway there. Oh contraire. Actually, this is where I tell you that there is no such thing as failure. What? *There is no such thing as failure.* It does not exist, and there is no way that you can fail in attempting to achieve your goals.

We (me included) all too often engage in the irrational thought process of "all or nothing" thinking. Do you remember this cognitive distortion? If not, here is a refresher: "This type of thinking sees the world in extremes. There is no middle ground with this type of thinking. You are either smart or stupid, skinny or fat, successful or a failure. One example would be if you started a new medication and began to feel better but not as well as you felt before you got sick, and so you tell yourself that the medicine has failed. Rational and realistic thinking can see the world from the middle and stay away from extremes." What we commonly refer to as failure is actually something of a misnomer. Life is a process, an ongoing and never-ending project as we search for meaning and satisfaction. *There are no mistakes, just lessons.*

Instead of seeing a shortcoming as a failure, see it as a learning opportunity. Otherwise, how else would we grow? This refers back to using the language of solutions as opposed to the language of problems. Instead of saying to yourself, "I failed," say, "What did I learn?" This simple turn of phrase in your mind can make all the difference in the world. What we see now as failures are simply opportunities for learning. Think about the last thing you attempted and fell short on. Now ask yourself, "What did I learn?" Can you see how much more productive and successful we can be if we saw failure as an opportunity?

Here is an example of the last thing I tried and fell short on: I wanted to be able to run five miles without stopping. This doesn't really sound like all that great a distance, but the truth is that I hate running. I hate it with a passion, and I'm not sure why. Even though I hate it with the fire of a thousand suns, I decided that I wanted to be able to run five miles because being able to run long distances is really cool to talk about with other fitness enthusiasts (I know, great motivation, right?). That wasn't my only reason though. I have always been lacking in the cardio department, and I had dedicated myself to improving upon my fitness weaknesses.

As a former fat guy, running any distance was a bit of a challenge, but I was determined. I did some research, made a plan, and started my journey to five miles within three months. I would set my alarm for five thirty in the morning, get up, and pound the pavement. If I missed a morning jog, I would catch up during lunch or after work. Man, I was religious about getting my running in. I was engaging people in conversations about jogging, nodding my head and pretending to agree whenever they said something like, "I just love running!" or, "Man, when I hit that runner's high after two miles…" or, my favorite, "I am so productive when I am running! My mind is free to be creative!" All I could think about while running was not throwing up and whether or not my jogging app would let me cheat to make it look as if I ran farther than I had. Yes, I know—I am a bad person. Even through all of that, I pressed on. I was "acting as if" I enjoyed running, and it was starting to work a little bit. I was well on my way to my goal until…life happened. It started innocently enough. I would miss one run here or there. My child was sick and I stayed home; I was bogged down in work; I overdid it running one day and was too sore to run the next. Almost suddenly, I was spending more days not running than running. The day I had set to achieve my goal came…and I had fallen short. Way short. There was no way I could run five miles without stopping. I had failed. Or had I?

Prior to starting this goal, I could run less than one mile without stopping, and now I could run about three. I also noticed that I begrudgingly started to like some things about running and even enjoyed parts of my run. What did I learn? I learned that committing to running every day is a difficult task, I may never enjoy running as much as other people, I need to reevaluate my commitment level for this goal, five miles is longer than I thought, and I can improve on my weaknesses.

# What If You Fail?

Would you say that I failed? Not by a longshot. Not reaching that goal was like a master class in life lessons, and I grew tremendously as a person. Challenge your perspective. Your failures are not failures at all. They are learning experiences. You may not reach your goals, and you may not even reach your objectives. That is OK because you have done *something*. Adjust, adapt, and grow. If you don't make it then change yourself or your goals to help you get there next time. If you are trying, you are growing.

---

### Thrive Thought:

Here comes the big secret of *The Thrive Life* (I had to put it toward the end to hide it from cheaters): living a thrive life is not about achieving goals. What? The *journey* is the thrive life, and as you progress you will realize that there is no such thing as arriving. When you achieve your goals—and you will—set new ones. Being in control of who you are and your life direction is what a thrive life is all about.

Don't overlook the process! We have become so results-oriented, so focused on what we do or do not achieve, that we forget the journey. Don't you see it? If you are trying, truly striving, then you are living a thrive life, my friend.

---

# CHAPTER 24

# Find Your Meaning

In part I of *The Thrive Life*, I discussed how our behaviors send out messages about who we are. All our behaviors send messages, whether we intend for them to or not. Our behavior messages say far more about who we are and what we care about than our words ever could. It was excruciating for me to look back on my life and realize what messages my behavior was sending, especially to the people I cared about the most. In parenthesis are the messages my behavior was sending: I am incredibly unhealthy (I don't care about my life or being alive long enough to be with you), I skip college to the point of being on academic probation (I do not care about my future or yours since our futures are intertwined), and I have no career ambitions (I do not care about providing for our family in the future). My entire lifestyle at that point could be summed up by the message "*I do not care about myself, I do not care about my family, and I prefer mediocrity.*" Wow...that is painful. Talk about a gut check. No, no, no—that cannot be right. That is certainly not how I felt, but who I was spoke louder than my words. My motivation, my ah-ha moment, my catalyst for change was the realization of my lifestyle message. It was not just the message; it was knowing that nothing I ever said would speak louder than my actions, and my actions were not saying what I wanted them to say.

## Thrive Work:

Take a good, long look at your goals (just the goals). Read over them slowly and carefully. Now imagine the messages you are sending to your loved ones and others by striving for and ultimately achieving your goals. For me, this was the ultimate motivator. Let's take a look at our example goals and see what messages they are sending to loved ones.

1. Be a better husband and father: I love you, and spending more time with you is the most important thing to me.
2. Achieve a graduate degree: it is important to strive to maximize your potential; I am reaching to be the best I can be.
3. Be healthier: taking care of your body is important; I want to live as long as possible to spend time with you.

Yes. Those are the messages that I want to send to my family and friends because that is how I really feel. The thought of my behaviors sending the opposite messages (they were) makes me sick. As you begin your journey toward becoming the best you, do not forget the other people in your life because your journey will have profound effects on them as well.

Your goals are what you are trying to achieve, and your objectives are how you will achieve them, but have you thought about your why? Maybe you haven't considered this yet, but it is at least as important as your what and how. Why do you want to achieve these goals? What meaning would this have for you in your life? Nietzsche said, "He who has a why can bear any how." This quote was never truer for anyone than it was for Viktor Frankl. Viktor Frankl was an Austrian psychiatrist who is credited as one of the leaders of existential therapy. He was a man who endured unspeakable horrors at the hands of the Nazis in their concentration camps and survived to tell the story. Frankl would go on to develop what he called "logotherapy." *Logo* comes from the Greek word that denotes "meaning," and so Frankl coined "meaning therapy." Frankl says in his book, *Man's Search for Meaning*, that striving to find meaning in life is humankind's primary motivation. He goes on to point out that large, burly men would enter the concentration camps, and everyone would think that these men were likely to survive. If anyone could endure the torture from the Nazis, surely it would be these giant, strong men. That was not the case though, as these men were the ones who seemed to fall the quickest. Frankl noticed a "giving up" by some people. Not that he faulted them for this, as they all contemplated giving up, but it was the people who managed to find some sort of meaning for their suffering who survived the longest. Frankl said, "What is to give light must endure burning," and no one can claim to have suffered more burning than Viktor Frankl himself. He lost his wife, mother, and many other loved ones in the camps.

How remarkable is it that in the face of one of the most terrible human tragedies such beautiful work as *Man's Search for Meaning* could appear? In his book, Frankl tackles the question that has plagued humankind since the beginning of time: what is the meaning of life? Frankl wrote:

*The meaning of life differs from man to man, from day to day, and from hour to hour. What matters, therefore, is not the meaning of life in general but rather the specific meaning of a person's life at a given moment. To put the question in general terms would be comparable to the question posed to a chess champion: "Tell me, master, what is the best move in the world?" There simply is no such thing as the best or even a good move apart from a particular situation in a game and the particular personality of one's opponent. The same holds for human existence. One should not search for an abstract meaning of life. Everyone has his own specific vocation or mission in life to carry out a concrete assignment which demands fulfillment. Therein he cannot be replaced, nor can his life be repeated. Thus, everyone's task is as unique as is his specific opportunity to implement it.*

*Ultimately, man should not ask what the meaning of his life is, but rather must recognize that it is he who is asked. In a word, each man is questioned by life; and he can only answer to life by answering for his own life; to life he can only respond by being responsible.*

*The Thrive Life* is not about theology, philosophy, or religion; please don't misunderstand me. The fact remains, however, that unless you have a "why," you are unlikely to get to your "what." The message from the above passage is clear and something I firmly believe: there is no abstract, write-it-down meaning of life for everyone. You have your own meaning because your life is contextual, and your meaning is ever-shifting based on that context. What is the difference between survivors of horrific events who are motivated to do great things and those who use the event as a crutch for an unsatisfactory life? One is able to find meaning; the other is not. Or, to put it in choice theory verbiage, one *chooses* to find meaning and the other *chooses* not to find meaning.

## Thrive Work:

This is the last exercise and probably the most important. Look at your goals again—just the goals. Pull them out and read them over. Next to them write the "why" each goal has for your life. Your reasons do not have to be altruistic and noble. It is OK if your "why" for getting in shape is to look better in a bathing suit. Just make sure you have a "why." Here is my example.

# Find Your Meaning

1. Be a better husband and father: I want my spouse and children to know how much they really mean to me, and I want my children to grow up to be loving and respecting givers to society.
2. Achieve a graduate degree: I want to achieve my full potential and be great at something. I want to leave a lasting impression with my work.
3. Be healthier: I want to look good, and I enjoy the self-confidence I feel when I look good. I also want to live as long as I possibly can, to grow old with my wife, and to spend time with my grandchildren.

This is it, folks. Your "why" is the last piece you need. This is where you will find your ultimate motivation to achieve your goals. Remember your "whys" when you are tired, weak, and beaten down. Your goals should be difficult, and they should stretch you, but they will not break you. I said *they will not break you!* Your "why" will be the reason you wake up at five in the morning to exercise. Your "why" will be the reason you sacrifice sleep for studying. Your "why" will be the reason you stand up and say, "Enough! I am tired of how my life has been lived, and I am ready for a change!" Now is the time to choose a more effective way of life. You have all of the tools you need. Grab the steering wheel of your total behavior car, point it in the direction of your goals, and put your foot on the gas pedal…today.

# References

Frankl, V. E. (1984). *Man's Search for Meaning.* New York: Washington Square Press.

Siegel, D. J. (2012). *Pocket Guide to Interpersonal Neurobiology: An Integrative Handbook of the Mind.* New York: W.W. Norton & Company.

Wubbolding, R. E. (2000). *Reality Therapy for the 21st Century.* Bridgeport, New Jersey: Taylor & Francis.